John Day Fossil Beds National Monument

Museum Management Plan

Recommended by:

_____ May 15, 2008
Diane L. Nicholson   Date
Regional Curator, Pacific West Region

Concurred by:

_____ 5/21/2008
Jim Hammett   Date
Superintendent, John Day Fossil Beds National Monument

Approved by:

_____ 7/14/2008
Jonathan B. Jarvis   Date
Regional Director, Pacific West Region

John Day Fossil Beds National Monument

Museum Management Planning Team

Carola DeRooy, Archivist
Point Reyes National Seashore
Point Reyes, California

Greg McDonald, Ph.D, Senior Curator of Natural History
Park Museum Management Program
National Park Service
Fort Collins, Colorado

Steve Floray, Curator
Pacific West Region
Thousand Oaks, California

Herbert W. Meyer, Ph.D, Paleontologist
Florissant Fossil Beds National Monument
Florissant, Colorado

Ted Fremd, Curator and Chief of Paleontology
John Day Fossil Beds National Monument
Kimberly, Oregon

Diane L. Nicholson, Regional Curator
Pacific West Region
Oakland, California
(Team Leader)

Sally Shelton, Collections Officer
National Museum of Natural History
Smithsonian Institution
Washington, D.C.

Department of the Interior
National Park Service
Pacific West Region
2008

Executive Summary

The John Day Fossil Beds National Monument Museum Management Plan identifies a series of collections management issues facing the park and presents corresponding actions to address them.

This plan represents a snapshot of the park during a two-week visit in June 2007 and makes recommendations based on the team's observations and interactions with park staff. Since that visit the park has made a number of changes and has implemented a number of those recommendations. Most notably, a park collections manager was selected and began work in March 2008.

According to the 2007 Collections Management Report (CMR), the park has a collection numbering almost 58,000 items in 355 accessions. The vast majority are paleontological specimens (more than 45,000). Although the park was created to preserve, research, and interpret its significant paleontological collections, John Day Fossil Beds National Monument (JODA) also has significant cultural and other natural resources.

Cultural resource collections include archeology and history items. The 2007 CMR indicates that there are about 4,500 archeological items and 1,561 history items. The increased number for archeological items (in 2006 the number was only 116) is based upon information gained during the course of this plan but largely consists of debitage and unidentifiable bone fragments. As more research is conducted, the value and significance of this collection grows and indicates a human habitation of approximately 10,000 years. The historical materials are related to the Cant Ranch and the Cant-Mascall families but many of these artifacts are on temporary loan. The Cant Ranch is representative of the sheep/cattle ranching history of central Oregon and provides a context for the early history of the expeditions that first explored the area for its paleontological resources.

Although the CMR identifies only about 3,000 archives items, much of the park's archival collections, including resource management records, oral histories, and documentation related to paleontological resources has not been moved into the park archives. These materials provide context for and additional information about the park and all its resources. The archives will undoubtedly grow as more attention is paid to it.

Biological and geological collections number about 3,500 items; however, based on the information gathered during this plan, there are biological collections completed during early surveys as well as more recent inventory and monitoring programs which have not been added to the park collection.

Early management of the park had intended that paleontological research be done under agreements through the Cooperative Park Study Units (CPSUs) and that specimens would be housed at those institutions. But in the early 1980s this changed with the beginning of the research and curatorial programs at the park. As noted in the collections history chapter of this plan, museum collecting began soon after the park was created in 1976. Early collections were mainly loaned historical materials related to the Cant Ranch. The park collection numbers in various reports, however, do not include recent archeological nor archival collections, including administrative history and all of the field documentation. In addition, some unaccessioned cultural and natural resource collections need to be reviewed for possible addition to the museum collection.

There are four main repositories outside the park that house John Day Basin paleontological collections: the American Museum of Natural History in New York; the Peabody Museum at Yale which houses the Yale and Princeton collections; the Burke Museum, University of Washington; and the University of California, Berkeley, Museum of Paleontology. In addition, about ten repositories throughout the United States house smaller collections. Finally, collections are also to be found in Great Britain and elsewhere in Europe. All of these historical collections were made prior to the establishment of the park but contain important type specimens from the Basin.

Opened in 2003, with museum exhibits opening in 2005, the Thomas Condon Paleontology Center hosts the park visitor center as well as paleontological collections and accessions storage, paleontology laboratory, and staff offices. The paleontology laboratory has a window which faces onto the main visitor center area, allowing park visitors to view preparators working with specimens. Natural resource, cultural resource, and archival collections are located in the third floor of the Cant Ranch House.

The paleontology program at John Day Fossil Beds coordinates and disseminates information concerning the geological and paleontological resources of the John Day Basin, including fossilized remains in the field and in the museum collection, and research concerning them. In general, the activities can be subdivided into eight areas:

- Professional operations include coordinating publications by scientists at a variety of institutions, performing services as peer reviewers, participating with professional societies, and other functions.

- Research activities important to the understanding of the fossilized biotas and interpretation of the ancient ecosystems include work in dozens of related disciplines, in the field, laboratory, and collections.

- Fieldwork and resource management functions involve the prospecting and retrieval or stabilization of scientifically significant fossil materials located in over 750 major localities cooperatively managed on various public lands.

- Paleontology, almost entirely a collections-based discipline, involves accessioning, cataloging, identification, and analysis of collections.

- Interpretive support consists of direct and indirect involvement of paleontology staff providing accessible information concerning the resource, ranging from short written essays to major exhibits, to various audiences.

- Laboratory work includes the careful exhumation of the fossilized remains from the entombing rock; consolidation, stabilization, and preservation of all of the fossils; as well as the preparation of casts, thin sections, and other accessories.

- Servicewide activities include sharing the John Day Fossil Beds paleontological expertise with other NPS parks in the system that lack a major program; this includes the Science Advisor function and implementation of national paleobiology efforts.

Administrative tasks, including planning and cooperative functions with other agencies, participation with other institutions, and intra-park budgetary concerns are required to coordinate the functions listed above.

This Museum Management Plan offers recommendations for actions designed to take the park archives, library, and museum collections through the next developmental phase, leading to full program integration.

Key Recommendations

The key recommendations are listed here, while more detailed action recommendations follow each issue section of the plan.

- Fill the Collections Manager position to manage all park museum collections and functions. [Filled March 2008]

- Request the PWR Cultural Resource Advisory Committee's assistance in reviewing the park's cultural resource program fund requests.

- Update programming documents to address needed projects (PMIS) and operational increases (OFS).

- Improve information management tools and access procedures that promote intellectual and physical access to the resources in the park archives, library, and museum collections.

- Develop environmental and pest monitoring programs to assist in the preservation of park museum and archival collections.

- Refine collections storage areas in both the TCPC and the Cant Ranch House to use space more efficiently and provide for increase of collections for the next five years.

- Revise Scope of Collection Statement, acquisition plans, and paleontology program research plan to adequately address what the park will be collecting and estimate the amount of growth of the museum collections.

- Develop a policy for collecting materials from outside the park for interpretation and education that ensures that these materials do not become part of the park museum collection.

- Review agricultural implements currently not part of the museum collection for significance and find other homes for those not related to the Cant Ranch.

Table of Contents

Executive Summary 5
Key Recommendations 8
Table of Contents 9
Introduction 11
History of the Museum Collection 15
Recommendations 33
Issue A—Museum Management 35
Issue Statement 35
Background 35
Discussion 39
Recommendations 52
Issue B—Information Management 55
Issue Statement 55
Background 55
Discussion 63
Recommendations 70
Issue C—Collections Preservation 73
Issue Statement: 73
Background 73
Discussion 75
Recommendations 93
Issue D—Collections Development 95
Issue Statement 95
Background 95
Discussion 98
Recommendations 106
Appendix A—Archives, Library, and Museum Collections Survey Results .. 109
Appendix B—Suggested Workload Analysis 115
Appendix C—Possible Non-NPS Funding Sources 119
Appendix D—Preliminary Survey of Park Archives 123
Appendix E—NPS Records Management 127
Appendix F—Preparing Inactive Records for Transfer to Storage 133
Appendix G—Archiving Transfer of Resource Management Field Records to Museum Archives 141
Attachment A: Five Phases of Managing Archival Collections 148
Attachment B: Sample Archival and Manuscript Collections Survey Form .. 149
Appendix H—Suggested Collections Access Policies 151
Bibliography 167

List of Illustrations

Figure 1, page 14 - Cant Ranch House, built in 1917, now houses cultural resource exhibits, park administration offices, and cultural museum collections in the third floor attic. 2007

Figure 2, page 14 - Superb skull with associated postcrania of the primitive canid Mesocyon (JODA 761); collected outside park boundaries

Figure 3, page 34 - Paleontology storage

Figure 4, page 34 - Furnished parlor, first floor Cant Ranch House

Figure 5, page 61 - Cant Ranch House, 3rd floor permanent collection storage Room; temporary records also stored here

Figure 6, page 72 - Truck in field behind Cant Ranch Barn showing adaption for use as a crane; not museum item, 2007

Figure 7, page 72 - Preparator Matt Smith in paleontology lab on view to visitors in Thomas Condon Paleontology Center, 2007

Figure 8 - page 108 – JODA Library

List of Tables

Table 1, page 76 - Temperature range at JODA (outdoors)

Table 2, page 77 - JODA annual precipitation

Table 3, page 92 - Cost estimates for common environmental monitoring supplies

Table 4, page 96 - Number of JODA cataloged items in each discipline

Table 5, page 99 - Number of cataloged paleontological and geological specimens in JODA collections from 2000 to 2006 based on park-submitted CMR

Table 6, page 102 - Number of cataloged items of biology, archeology, history, and archive records in JODA collections from 2000 to 2006 based on park-submitted CMR

Introduction

Within the Pacific West Region, the Museum Management Plan (MMP) replaces the Collection Management Plan (CMP) referred to in National Park Service publications such as the *Outline for Planning Requirements; DO#28: Cultural Resource Management*; and the *NPS Museum Handbook*. Whereas the CMP process generally concentrates on the technical aspects of archival and museum operations, the MMP recognizes that specific directions for these technical aspects already exist in the *NPS Museum Handbook* series.

The MMP process therefore does not duplicate that information. Instead it places archival and museum operations in a holistic context within park operations by focusing on how collections may be used by park staff to support specific park goals. This plan recognizes that there are many different ways in which archives, libraries, and museum collections may be organized, linked, and used within individual parks, and as a result provides park-specific advice on how this may be accomplished within this specific unit. Where necessary, material found in the *NPS Museum Handbook* or *Conserve O Gram* series will be referenced in the text, and where required, technical recommendations not covered will appear as appendices to this plan.

The John Day Basin was first recognized as an important paleontological site in the 1860s, thanks to the ability of a young frontier minister, Thomas Condon, who recognized the fossil beds as a scientific treasure. By the late 19th Century, researchers at Yale, Princeton, and the Smithsonian Institution had requested and received hundreds of specimens from the John Day Basin. This early work set the stage for field paleontologists such as John C. Merriam, who in 1889 began the task of placing the John Day fossils in their geological, chronological, and paleoecological context. His efforts were instrumental in the preservation of this area.

John Day Fossil Beds National Monument (JODA) was authorized as part of an omnibus bill, October 24, 1974, PL 93-486: "(2) for establishment as the John Day Fossil Beds National Monument, Oregon...." The legislation provides no further guidance on the park other than it was to name the principle visitor center after Thomas Condon. There were a number of documents created both before and after the legislation that provided guidance for park management and preservation (see *Floating in the Stream of Time: An Administrative History of John Day Fossil Beds National Monument*, 1996).

The park mission statement, "The purpose of John Day Fossil Beds National Monument is to preserve, and provide for the scientific and public understanding of, the paleontological resources of the John Day region and natural, scenic, and cultural resources within the boundaries of the national monument[,]" clearly provides the foundation for the park museum program and leads to the significance statements developed for the Draft General Management Plan (2007).

The park staff and the MMP team worked together over the course of the site visit to develop the issue statements contained in this plan. Topics addressed meet the specific need of John Day Fossil Beds National Monument as discussed during those meetings, and thus do not necessarily represent a complete range of collections management concerns. Most elements of this plan are developmental rather than remedial in nature. The recommendations are intended to guide the park through the process of creating and implementing a workable system that supports all aspects of park operations, while at the same time providing guidelines for the growth and development of the museum management program.

Members of the MMP team were selected for their ability to address specific needs and concerns of the park. Primary information gathering and the initial draft were developed over a two-week period in June 2007.

The team wishes to thank Superintendent Jim Hammett and the staff of John Day Fossil Beds National Monument for the courtesy, consideration, and cooperation extended during this planning effort, in particular Paleobotanist Regan Dunn and Preparator Matt Smith from the paleontology/museum program, Park Ranger Lia Vella, who provided useful comments, and Park Ranger Sarah Herve, who provided, amongst other assistance, the photographs and map for the plan. Their time, efforts, and involvement greatly facilitated the work, and are very much appreciated. These individuals obviously are dedicated and committed to the preservation of the park resources, and it is a pleasure to work with such professionals.

Figure 1   Cant Ranch House, built 1917, now houses cultural resource exhibits, park administration offices, and cultural museum collections in the third floor attic. 2007

Figure 2   Superb skull with associated postcrania of the primitive canid Mesocyon (JODA 761); collected outside park boundaries

History of the Museum Collection

Perspective

The real significance of the John Day Fossil Beds National Monument is not easily conveyed to the general public, NPS employees, or even curatorial personnel. Unlike some of the more physically spectacular areas administered by the National Park Service, such as Yellowstone or the Grand Canyon, places like JODA are very subtle. In the deafening world of the present, these are the quiet, almost delicate chimes of deep time. They don't have the sudden clamor about them that signals to most people "Wow, look at this ... this is important." There are no enormous canyons, tidewater glaciers, or towering redwood trees. But the resources preserved in this volcanic wonderland of the past are among the more meaningful in the National Park system. The museum collections are central to the understanding, preservation, and appreciation of these resources—indeed, few other disciplines are as completely reliant on the museum function as paleontology.

John Day Basin does not have a mere bed of fossils, but an entire sequence of beds of fossils, spanning 40 million years of time. Altogether, probably thousands of discrete beds containing evidence of the past form a composite section a mile thick spread over 10,000 square miles. Fossils are carefully removed from these beds and then are "prepared"—that is, the encapsulating rock (usually distinctive volcaniclastic sediment) is painstakingly removed from the specimens by skilled technicians. They are then identified and cataloged into the National Park Service museum system, where scholars can examine them with their associated records. Systematically ordered, carefully documented collections such as these are the data from which hypotheses are tested and theories of Earth's past are formulated. Every specimen, however large or small, is a piece of information that potentially can solve or add to some of the mysteries of the past. The challenge for the curator is to anticipate research questions from a very wide spectrum of disciplines and investigators.

Perhaps the most surprising aspect of the strata within the John Day Basin is the large number of localities and horizons deposited in a diverse variety of depositional environments. Six of these major locality assemblages / episodes of the region's life/paleontological history are currently protected within the boundaries of the national monument or on proximal federal lands. To see all of these deposits in one place, and add to them the remarkable intervening strata, is very unusual in North American (if not global) Tertiary terrestrial basins. The early museum collections developed by several major institutions were largely made prior to this understanding.

There are no *lagerstätten* sites (i.e., fossil localities that have exceptional completeness and diversity, and a high quality of preservation) similar to the Canadian Burgess shales, the Liaoning deposits of China, the Messel in Germany, or other such classic well-preserved "time capsules" or even bone beds that lead to the creation of other NPS fossil parks such as Dinosaur, Agate, or Hagerman Fossil Beds. Why, then, is this area so important? Not only are fossils well preserved here, but they are very diverse, are preserved in many different kinds of sediments and paleoecosystems, span a much longer time period than any *lagerstätten* possibly could, and are bracketed by a profusion of high-quality synchronous tuffs. The existence of a systematic paleontological museum collection with stratigraphic integrity, well-curated associated records and field archives, and an associated laboratory equipped to prepare, stabilize, and replicate unique fossils provides the necessary system to properly store and retrieve large quantities of high-quality research data.

Early Discovery and Initial Collections

While there are anecdotal records of American Indians retrieving and storing in pit houses fossil leaves from the Bridge Creek strata, the first efforts to collect fossils for scientific study in the John Day region dates back to Civil War days. A variety of detailed narratives describe many of the efforts from this era, so it is unnecessary to enumerate much of this historic effort here. But it is interesting that the fossils that drew Thomas Condon's attention were retrieved by members of the U. S. Cavalry; these encouraged him to make the first of many collecting expeditions into the area.

Condon's keen interest in paleontology certainly paved the way for efforts by what were then the great paleontological institutions of the East to visit and accumulate specimens from the area. The fossil horse specimens that Condon collected and sent to Othniel Charles Marsh at Yale, for example, became the key specimens that were used to delineate the evolutionary "tree" of horse family. This was the first such documentation of the phylogeny of a lineage ever assembled, and a largely overlooked role of the Basin's fossils in the development of evolutionary thinking.

Thus, the John Day fossil collections were recognized as important, if unheralded, physical objects or artifacts in a historical context tied to the very beginnings of the events that led to our modern understanding of the evolutionary process. Condon sent vertebrate specimens to some of the giants of paleontology of the day, including Cope, Leidy, Osborn, and others. Condon's fossil plant specimens were studied by J.S. Newberry, and a collection of fossil plants made by C. D. Voy about 1870 were studied by Leo Lesquereux; these studies represent some of the pioneering work in American Tertiary paleobotany.

Numerous other collectors visited for short periods of time, amassing significant material currently stored off-continent (such as the specimens from Lord Walsingham's expedition). The remoteness of the area, rarity of complete mammalian skeletons, and matrices that are very difficult to remove from the specimens, however, were factors in making the John Day a less desirable destination than the Big Badlands of South Dakota or the Bridger Basin in Wyoming.

The most important collections to be made in the John Day Basin in the late 1800s contain many of the species holotypes (over 150) which unfortunately lack any precise locality, much less stratigraphic, data. These include the spectacular specimens currently housed in the Frick Building of the American Museum of Natural History, largely under the direction of Edward Drinker Cope; the material collected by Othniel Charles Marsh and his workers for the Yale Peabody Museum; a large number of specimens retrieved during an expedition by William Berryman Scott in 1889; the C. D. Voy collection at the University of California Museum of Paleontology; Condon's fossil plant collection at the National Museum of Natural History; and the thousands of specimens retrieved by John C. Merriam of the University of California Museum of Paleontology.

Most of the vertebrate collections have been carefully studied by JODA staff and detailed records of the material are recorded in archives and photographed. The collections stored at other museums were NPS-assessed in order to ascertain the diversity and relative abundance of taxa and skeletal material. This was required to provide a baseline for distinguishing scientifically significant material from the commonplace during fieldwork such as cyclic prospecting. It also was important to examine existing collections to develop the necessary collection of reference casts in order to facilitate identification of new material, determine the extent of collecting biases in the early methodologies, and to plan suitable exhibits.

Development of Methodologies

Probably one of the most important periods in the development of John Day collections began in the early 1900s with the arrival of John C. Merriam and his efforts to systematically describe the paleontology of the region without simply resorting to "trophy" collecting of skulls.

The John Day Associates was a brainstorm of Merriam, who was with U. C. Berkeley and was one-time president of the Carnegie Institute of Washington. The Associates consisted of many top regional scientists belonging to a variety of disciplines, gathered together in the 1920s by Professor Merriam to study the attributes of the John Day Valley.

Merriam's role in the John Day Basin cannot be overstated. He provided the first really comprehensive understanding of the geology, described many important new species, compiled authoritative faunal lists for the first time, and published exceptional manuscripts on the area. One of the most influential people to work in the John Day, he spent years studying this area and felt it was one of the outstanding places on Earth for several reasons. Merriam writes: "...acquaintance with the John Day Valley contributes three things of exceptional importance: first, the view of a *spectacular scenic area*; second, some understanding of *problems involved in building of the earth;* and, third, a *vision of the history of life and its evolution* seen in relation to the processes of earth building and shaping."[1]

From ca. 1900 to 1940, the collections were largely made by Merriam and his colleagues, including paleobotanist F. H. Knowlton and Ralph W. Chaney and other paleontologists such as Eustace Furlong, Chester Stock, R. A. Stirton, and others. Chaney, in particular, became a noteworthy contributor, and his work on the Bridge Creek flora is thought to be the very first fieldwork that developed models of quantitative paleoecology. During a brief collecting interval he acquired more than 20,000 specimens from a small hill. Vertebrate paleontologists from California Institute of Technology (CIT) and other institutions often made use of local expertise, such as the collections acquired from the Weatherford family that were retrieved from the exposures of the Mascall and Rattlesnake strata.

At the time of its authorization in 1974, three state parks formed the heart of John Day Fossil Beds National Monument. Although the state's priorities for park development generally lay in other parts of Oregon, it acquired parkland in the upper John Day Basin over a 40 year period.

From 1940 through 1980, one could typify the events as being in the "Chaney through Rensberger" era, with important collections made by Thomas Bones, Lon Hancock, John Rensberger, Morton Green, Ted Downs, and others. The discovery of tremendously important nuts, seeds, and leaves from the Clarno Nut Beds catapulted the Clarno area into the "world-class" locality arena, with hundreds of species of paratropical forest plants, including trees and lianas, fortuitously encapsulated in a series of lahars (volcanic mudflows). Recent studies demonstrate that this locality's fossil woods alone merit global recognition, as they represent one of the most diverse sites (and *the* most diverse published site).

---

[1] J. C. Merriam, "Paleontological, Geological, and Historical Research," Carnegie Institute of Washington Yearbook 43 (1944): 195.

Unfortunately, many of these specimens have been lost to science, although the two largest collections in the world (at the Smithsonian and at JODA) are in the public domain.

Subsequent and fortuitous discoveries of the remarkable bone-bed of Eocene mammals at the Hancock Mammal Quarry revealed one of the finest sites of this age, populated by extraordinary species. Three of these taxa have recently (2006) been recognized as entirely new to science. A large backlog of specimens collected in conjunction with the Oregon Museum of Science and Industry's Paleontology Research Team at Camp Hancock during 1969 to 1972 and housed for decades on the campus of the University of California, Berkeley (UCMP) awaits preparation by the JODA laboratory during the tenure of long-term loans. It is likely more new taxa are currently encapsulated in these plaster jackets.

Although by far the majority of mammalian fossils in historical collections were retrieved from the blue-green beds of the Turtle Cove strata of the John Day sequence, largely in rocks dated between 29 and 25 million years ago, a variety of collections have been made from the younger sediments deposited after the cessation of the Picture Gorge Basalts, ca. 16 million years ago. The Mascall Formation turns out to be much thicker than previously thought (thus spanning a longer time range, including an important global climate event known as the mid-Miocene Climatic Optimum, or MMCO). Fossil plants from the formation provide important information for interpreting the paleoclimate during this time.

The formation also includes important records of early "elephants," the adaptive radiation of horses, "giraffe-deer" and pronghorns, canids, and many other mammals. It is sufficiently distinctive that a "Mascallian" North American Land Mammal Age (NALMA) has been proposed and periodically is suggested. The youngest nationally significant strata in the park, the Rattlesnake strata, have yielded important records of latest Miocene mammals and the type area within the park boundaries is considered one of the principal correlates of the Hemphillian NALMA. Many of these collections were made in the 1970s, prior to the establishment of the park, and are stored at such far-flung repositories as the South Dakota School of Mines and Technology.

The fate of non-vertebrate fossil collections is less certain. Geologic collections, made by early students of volcaniclastics such as Richard Hay and Richard Fisher, apparently have not been cataloged. Large collections of varied John Day fossil floras are maintained at the UCMP, including good specimens from the Mascall and Bridge Creek floras. Most of these were collected using classic quarrying techniques that made no attempt to minimize the effect of "time-averaging," and a single quarry was assumed to represent a discrete point in time and a single ecosystem. Current work demonstrates that, in fact, most floras of the Oligocene/Miocene were no where near as speciose as thought and historic interpretations of paleobiomes, such as Chaney's comparison of the Bridge Creek to the environment of the modern Muir Woods, have shown to be incorrect. Yet more unfortunately, critical field notes that may have been kept by early workers have not been located, and their original field observations may be irretrievable.

NPS Involvement

A movement to establish the area as a national park predates the National Park Service. For example, the Dec 1, 1916 issue of the county newspaper, the *Blue Mountain Eagle*, contains a recommendation for park status that includes "The famous fossil beds of the John Day Valley ... should never be turned over to private speculators, but should belong to the people. It might be well for the government to withhold the lands from entry and establish here a national park." That action did not happen until 60 years later, during which interval the area was part of the Oregon State Park system.

Surprisingly, the first museum work associated with the park was not with the nationally significant paleontologic resources for which it was established. The administrative history of the park suggests that NPS representatives made a variety of verbal assurances to the descendants of the Cant family, including a pledge that the cultural history of the area would receive interpretive attention after the ranch house and environs was purchased.

With the establishment of the national monument in 1975, the park purchased significant portions of the historic Cant Ranch, including a well-preserved ca. 1918 ranch house, largely to acquire a centralized infrastructure to facilitate administrative activities. It followed that early development of displays included a desire to furnish one or more rooms with authentic historic pieces. Thus the first park accession was a loan of some furnishings from Lillian Cant Mascall (that was creatively used to decorate a parlor by Jean Swearingen, then an interpretive planner at DSC, and the first collections specialist to work with the park).

Although the first NPS historic themes studies did not even mention sheep ranching as an important component of the park's cultural story, with the nomination and listing of the James Cant Ranch Historic District to the National Register of Historic Places in 1984, that theme has arguably gained pre-eminence at the present time. According to that nomination, written by Dr. Stephanie Toothman, the Cant Ranch has been a local landmark in the John Day River Valley since the construction of the main ranch house. It may be one of the most intact remaining examples of early 20th century ranching operations and demonstrates the transition from sheep to cattle ranch over the life of the ranch.

The museum collections relating to the history of the ranch and the Cant family are small in number and a large part are under a loan which is currently out of date due to the death of the lender, and the inheritor may choose to reclaim them. Farm implements and other equipment are also housed either in the barn or on display out-of-doors within the boundaries of the ranch. Some of these are museum property and some are park property. Preservation and protection of these materials are a challenge for the park.

Additional cultural themes associated with the archeological record have been described in a variety of cultural resource reports. There have been several surveys of various parts of the park. Some of these materials are accessioned and under the control of the National Park Service, although presently not located at JODA, and others need to be brought into the museum system. The most recent collection is currently located at Mount

Rainier National Park where it was analyzed, processed, and cataloged. It will eventually be returned to the park.

The cultural collections were somewhat problematic, in that large numbers of unsecured piles of artifacts with uncertain provenance were placed in the barn by the family and their associates. Prior to hiring the museum specialist, many objects were simply discarded (B. Ladd, personal communication). Desirous of doing the right thing, but ignorant of unbiased historical perspectives, the park decided to contract with a qualified non-NPS historian to at least establish the parameters within which the museum staff could make rational decisions concerning these items.

The park was well-served by consultants from the Oregon State Historic Preservation Office (SHPO), and furnished with a plan for dealing with much of the material. It was decided to break the artifacts into "significant or insignificant" categories, and place the former into three groups: locally, regionally, and nationally significant. All of the nationally significant (extremely rare), some of the regionally important material, and none of the locally significant artifacts were recommended to be cataloged. This resulted in approximately 300 historic objects added to the previous (loaned) collections. Currently, there is no effort to acquire more museum property in this category; indeed, return of the loaned artifacts from the Mascall family may be appropriate. At this writing, the cultural collections located in the park are stored on the third floor of the Cant Ranch in the midst of the historic fabric of which they form a portion.

Biologic specimens have a similar checkered background, beginning with a variety of study skins, isolated skulls, and "butterflies" collected by natural-history oriented staff, for the purposes of interpretation but not as part of any integrated scientific survey or inventory. In recent years, several small collections of natural history specimens—including aquatic insects, moths, and plant voucher specimens—have been added on an intermittent basis. A number of these collections are currently located at repositories which need to be accounted for.

The park's first museum specialist (paleontologist) was hired in June, 1984; prior to that time the park interpretive staff dealt with collections. At that time the collections amounted to approximately 300 fossil specimens, many of which were the Nut Beds material purchased from Tom Bones, and a small collection of vertebrates which were stored in a closet in the interpreter's residence in the Foree region of the Sheep Rock Unit. An unaccessioned collection of approximately 1,000 specimens retrieved under a contract with a department member at Oregon State University was among the first curatorial tasks undertaken by the park at this time.

The decision to house fossil specimens at the park was not made immediately, and some discussions concerning curating the materials at other repositories was inevitable. The later thinking of curatorial staff is reflected in the following excerpt concerning Hagerman Fossil Beds National Monument (HAFO) collections, certainly applicable to JODA (Fremd, letter to Hawkes, 10 Apr 1990).

> If the legislation calls for a research center, then the issue of whether or not specimens should be stored on-site becomes less controversial. Facilities normally required include preparation equipment and space, computer facilities ranging from simple word processors through access to proprietary literature databases to complex GIS systems, access to a reasonably adequate library and references collection, and - obviously - the original material. I suspect you will receive a wide variety of opinion on the latter: most museum-oriented staff would prefer not to see collections fragmented any further than they already are, and we don't need yet another repository. Conversely, most serious students of a fauna are arguably negligent if they fail to visit a classic area such as this; their job is that much easier if a disproportionate number of specimens are housed at the site. I think that a collection of material retrieved since establishment of the monument, with reference casts of earlier material, in close association with and proximity to the original sediments, is of immense value to taphonomists and paleoecologists and should be developed.

In 1988, then-Regional Director Charles Odegaard commented favorably and signed off on a document unique to the NPS up to that time: a *Paleontology Research Plan*. This called for, among other things, establishment of a well-studied, systematically stored museum collection that would be the source of unrivalled accuracy for John Day fossil specimens and their occurrence. This, as well as more than 25 other recommended strategies for elevating the monument's paleontological documentation and value, was carried out over the next decade. As a result of cyclic prospecting, paleontological reconnaissance, and prospecting at a wide variety of localities under interagency agreements (and other accession methods), the collection grew more than two-hundred fold to its current size (over 50,000 objects) and status as the largest collection of stratigraphically documented fossils from the John Day region in the world. To put this in context, the famous Condon Museum at the University of Oregon contains less than 35,000 specimens, from numerous locations and ages, many of which have no verifiable precise locality data.

The geologic collections consisted originally of very limited and non-systematically collected rocks, peculiar samples of volcanic ash from the Mt. St. Helens eruption, material incorrectly identified as "rough-horny dinosaur skin," and other things opportunistically accessioned. The first serious geologic collections were made as a result of a large contract to systematically map and describe the Clarno and Painted Hills units of the park. The contract, with Erick Bestland and Greg Retallack of the University of Oregon, called for a carefully documented set of hand samples and corresponding thin sections. This suite of stratigraphically documented samples forms a "stratigraphic section in a specimen cabinet"—a relatively complete set of samples of most of the field-distinguishable lithogies, paleosols, and unique depositional intervals that have been categorized through various analytical techniques. Most of this collection, consisting of over 1,300 catalog numbers, has been carefully analyzed, thin-sectioned, and published in the peer-reviewed literature including a Geological Society of America *Special Paper*, coauthored by the curator.

At this writing, JODA's collection is nearing 60,000 cataloged objects and is expanding the paleontological collections as a result of yearly field retrieval of significant specimens. Approximately the same total amount of specimens is known to be scattered in four major holdings, the University of California Museum of Paleontology (UCMP), the University of Washington Burke Museum (UWBM), the American Museum of Natural History (AMNH), and the Yale Peabody Museum (YPM, which also contains the Princeton material collected by Scott). Smaller, but important, collections are also housed at the Los Angeles County Museum

(LACM), the Condon collection at the University of Oregon (UO), the South Dakota School of Mines and Technology (SDSM&T), the University of Nebraska State Museum (UNSM), the National Museum of Natural History (USNM, "the Smithsonian"), the University of Florida (UF), and other institutions. Information pertaining to these is available to park and external investigators through a variety of archives housed at the park, including detailed study reports of different institutions' collections. A concerted effort to completely catalog the missing details of all the JODA collections, including the valuable scientific archives, would yield an impressive storehouse of knowledge concerning the paleontological resources of the area.

The Thomas Condon Paleontology Center had its grand opening in August, 2005. This new facility finally provides the necessary infrastructure for professional research and curation. Designed as a field station in the midst of the "places of discovery," attention was paid to all of the procedures involved in the process of documenting and retrieving fossil material in the field and placing it into dedicated museum storage. Details range from a loading ramp in the rear of the building specifically designed for fossil transport, to an accessions area, a well-equipped laboratory, and the systematic storage area with excellent security and climate control functions. A growing research library with current holdings of about 14,000 technical reprints emphasizes the fact that science works by publishing research results and testable hypotheses in the professional literature, an effort of which current staff are mindful. The exhibit gallery offers multi-tiered information accessible to all levels of visitors, from illiterate observers through professional paleontologists. The addition of a multi-purpose theater space, a classroom, and a spacious lobby filled with accessory exhibits rounds out the structure.

Museum Management Philosophy

The basic principles for managing museum collections in national parks are not always well understood. Park managers, resource managers, and interpreters are often too busy with their specialties and daily work to fully consider the concepts and logistics governing collections management. It is easy for parks to fall short of developing a sound museum management program and, as a result, not realize the full benefit and value possible from their collections.

This section provides the following background information about museum collections:

- The purpose of museum collections
- How museum collections represent park resources
- Determining where to locate museum collections
- Establishing access, use, and management policies for collections
- Professionalism in collections management

Purpose of Museum Collections within National Parks

Museum collections always contain objects and specimens, and the data associated with them that provides context and scientific value. Most parks also administer their own archives and operate their own libraries. These functions are necessary to support the work of the organization as a whole. It is not unusual for these resources—archives, collections, and libraries—also to be accessible to the public.

Within national parks, museum collections (including archives) serve four basic functions:

- **Documentation of resources** – Park collections should serve as documentation of the physical resources of the park as well as the history of the park efforts to preserve and protect those resources.

- **Physical preservation and protection of resources** – Park collections should help preserve and protect park resources, not only by keeping the specimens and collections made to document the resources, but also by preserving the information about the individual items and the resource as a whole. This is central to the management of both natural and cultural material.

- **Research** – During documentation of collections, a park performs research to provide the background information used in cataloging. The park is also responsible for making this information available to legitimate research, catalyzing, or performing that research which itself leads to new discoveries about an individual item, or the park as a whole.

- **Public programs** – The park is responsible for using its collections to provide information to the public. Exhibits, publications, and interpretive programs are traditional means of supplying public information, but new technology has led to other communication methods, including electronic access through web sites and on-line databases.

Paleontological Collections

The science of paleontology provides important information that helps to satisfy our human desire to understand the history of life on Earth. Understanding the many changes in the diversity of life through time helps us to see that everything changes over time, and that change in our modern world is inevitable. Most of our knowledge of paleontology is based on the study of fossils and the geographic and geological context in which they are preserved. Fossils are the tangible evidence of past life and as such are non-renewable resources that preserve extinct biotic communities representing unique combinations of time and geography. The protection and long-term preservation of fossils, either in their natural setting or in museum collections, is critical because they are non-renewable resources.

Scientifically significant specimens are removed from their natural occurrence in rocks for various reasons, including:

- scientific research according to an approved research plan,
- the prevention of natural destruction by weathering and erosion, and

- the prevention of illegal removal.

In most cases, fossils that remain uncollected are not useful for research, and controlled collecting is usually prerequisite to the preparation and analysis that furthers the understanding of the history of life on Earth. Controlled scientific collecting involves prospecting and retrieval in the field, including careful record-keeping of locality data and stratigraphic context to assure that the scientific value of the fossils is retained during removal. Many fossil specimens require detailed and often time-consuming preparation in the laboratory in order to provide exposure and stabilization. Application of consolidants and adhesives may be needed to stabilize or restore the condition of certain specimens. Cataloging and storage in a museum collection assures that important data remain associated with the fossils and that this information is available to future researchers.

The value of maintaining paleontological collections is:

- to document stratigraphic occurrences of fossils, thus providing information about evolutionary change in particular groups of organisms through time;
- to provide secure storage for the important type specimens that were established to define new species in accordance with the rules of botanical and zoological nomenclature, thus preserving irreplaceable information about the characteristics of species;
- to assess morphological variability within particular species, as represented by multiple specimens of the same taxon;
- to provide specimens that can be analyzed to reconstruct ancient environments, climates, and the compositions of biotic communities; and
- to provide a source of material that can be used in developing exhibits and programs to educate the public.

How Collections Represent Park Resources

A park's museum, library, and archival collections provide different perspectives on its resources:

- The museum collections, which contain three-dimensional objects and specimens, represent the resources within the monument's scope of collections, from outcrops within the strata of interest. Examples of museum collections include: artifacts from archeological activities; biological, geological, and paleontological specimens and resulting reports from resource management projects; and paint samples and building fragments from restoration of historic structures.

- The park archives should contain files, manuscripts, personal papers, maps, building plans, and photos that document the history of park development and the management of park resources. Individual collections within the archives should further document the activities that created portions of the museum collections. Examples of park archives include: field journals and maps created while collecting botanical or paleontological specimens; photographs taken during historic structure work; maps and as-built drawings made during utility installation; and property, land, and water use agreements that document past acquisition and use of park lands.

- The park library should contain both recent and historically published, peer-reviewed literature and less formal reports and documents relating to park resources and their management. Examples might include: general literature concerning local history, flora, and fauna; specialized scientific studies relative to biota and archeological resources found in the park; circulating copies of all park specific planning documents; and trade, craft, and professional journals reflecting the need for park staff to remain current in their field.

Determining Where to Locate Park Collections

The *NPS Museum Handbook* should be used as a guideline for identifying locations of branch or satellite park collections, and establishing methodologies for their documentation, organization, storage, and use.

Centrally located collections are often most effective since they promote efficient use of space (particularly in terms of combining preparation and work areas). However, it may also be efficient operationally to split the collections among potential users (for example, the herbarium and insect collection going to separate branches for storage and use).

Branch or satellite collections are possible as long as proper preservation and security conditions are met, and the requisite work areas necessary for management and use are provided. Overall responsibility for documentation, preservation, and reporting should, however, remain vested in one curatorial lead position, no matter where branch collections are located.

Any decision to place NPS collections in branch or satellite collections in partner repositories should only be made when both the park and partner repository have clearly articulated the mutual responsibilities of each partner.

Establishing Access, Use and Management Policies

Access, use, and management policies define who can access the collections (both staff and public), what types of use are possible and under what conditions, policies and procedures for consumptive analysis, and how the collections should be managed. Desired outcomes or products should be identified as well; for example, the types of services that are desired by staff from the collections manager. Some examples might include production of overlays for buried utilities; production of CDs containing research done at the park; liberal access to botanical specimens for comparative studies; and inter-library loan services. Samples of access, use, and management policies are located in the appendices or may be obtained from the regional curator.

The park may wish to consider the use of focus group exercises to develop a number of park-specific documents, including a Role and Function Statement, for the combined collections. These would clearly state who is responsible for the development of a joint resource and how it will function to serve park-wide goals. Access and use policies should be defined and implemented. Responsibilities for development, documentation, and management of the resources should be defined in a formal position description and associated performance standards. These objectives must be fully defined in writing if they are to be accomplished in fact.

Professionalism

The management of archival, museum, and library collections requires the application of three different, but related, management philosophies and technological approaches. These disciplines each have two components: technical and professional. It is possible to be proficient in either one of these components without being functional in the other.

The primary difference between the technical and the philosophical lies not only in understanding how to apply the technology, but in being able to determine when, why, and which technologies need to be applied in any given situation. This ability can be called "professionalism," and it can be an elusive, difficult thing to define—probably because most practitioners of the curatorial craft possess varying degrees of facility with both the technological and the philosophical aspects of the work.

Professionalism does need to be practiced and exercised to develop properly. It is better fostered by mentoring, particularly in the early stages, for professionalism is difficult to develop in isolation. It takes fairly intimate association with a range of others working in the craft, so that the developing professional personality has a healthy range of philosophy, opinion, and action to model. Professionalism also needs to be maintained in much the same manner.

The management of park archives was added to park curatorial portfolios in the mid 1980s, and increasingly, many park curators also manage the individual park library program. This accretion of complex duties has to some extent resulted from the overall loss of permanent positions service-wide, and particularly within the parks. These factors are not likely to improve in the foreseeable future, so park management must ensure that each position is filled with the best qualified candidate available.

The professional series and journeyman level for the position of park curator is GS-1015-11. The GS-1016 series is the technician or specialist series, which is not expected to operate independently from professional oversight especially at the technician or GS-7 level. A GS-1015-11 or GS-1420-11 is required by qualification standards, service, and regional policy to manage independently a museum program and administer museum program funds. Parks that do not have a GS-1015-11 or GS-1420-11 position on staff need to provide this oversight through the use of an agreement for a curator-of-record. Pacific West Region requires this.

The paleontologist/curator at JODA is a GS-1015-13 and so meets these criteria. However, the everyday collections management duties are not his primary responsibilities. He is the park paleontologist and is mainly involved in research both in the field and in the laboratory. In addition, the paleontologist/curator at JODA has been designated the science advisor for paleontology for the Pacific West Region. About 25% of his time is spent in assisting and advising parks on paleontological concerns. Finally, the paleontologist/curator has an adjunct appointment at the University of Oregon and participates on graduate committees for Masters and Doctoral students in paleontology. The latter takes less than 5% of his time but is enormously valuable to the research program at the park as well as the National Park Service's role in educating future professionals.

Recommendations

- Create a focus group of senior staff representing all park divisions and branches to define what the collections should contain, how they should be managed and accessed most efficiently, and what products should be produced upon request.

- Define the role and function of the combined collections by formal statement, formal access policies, and formal methodologies for depositing collections material, archival information, and required literature into the collections.

- Assign responsibility for developing and managing the collections to a single administrative unit and individual with a written position description and performance standards.

- Identify possible cooperative partnerships within the profession, park network, and in the community with individuals and groups that hold common interests regarding the preservation and management of park resources.

- Analyze the workload for the paleontological and museum program to determine the appropriate positions needed.

Figure 3 Paleontology storage

Figure 4 Furnished parlor, first floor Cant Ranch House

Issue A—
Museum Management

Issue Statement

Appropriate staffing, management, organization, planning, and security of the museum collections will facilitate the park's mission and goals.

Background

John Day Fossil Beds National Monument, established in 1975, is a rich paleontological resource composed of three separate units totaling 14,000 acres. Paleontology is the park's *raison d'être*. Subsequently, the park's most important resources are paleontological collections, museum specimens previously recovered from the park and surrounding lands as well as untold millions of unknown fossils remaining *in situ* in volcaniclastic sediments sandwiched between basalt flows, welded tuffs, and pyroclastic flows.

In FY 2007, the JODA budget is $1,353,000 of which about 18% or $252,463 is for the Division of Research. It is difficult to determine what part of that budget is for museum collections management per se but none is currently being used for a dedicated collections manager. These funds cover the salaries of the chief of Research, as well as those of the paleobotanist and the fossil preparator. Future budget development should anticipate costs associated with expendable supplies, permanent collection storage equipment to house the growing collections, and support.

The museum collection, which includes over 45,000 paleontological specimens representing 45 million years of earth's history, reflects the park's incalculable wealth of paleontological specimens and related scientific data. Based on data in the park's 2007 Collection Management Report (CMR), the entire museum collection consists of 58,686 specimens, artifacts, and archival materials which document the park's natural and cultural history. Smaller collections of archival, biological, geological, and history items are in addition to the paleontological specimens, which comprise 85% of the total museum collection. (Archival collections at the park are currently vastly underestimated, therefore the archival backlog is certainly greatly underreported on the 2006 CMR.)

Museum collections are located in two structures at the park, the Thomas Condon Paleontology Center and the Cant Ranch House. The Thomas Condon Paleontology Center, the park's primary visitor services, museum, and research facility, was completed by the park in 2004. The Paleontology Center houses a state-of-the-art paleontology museum that appeals to all ages, a collections storage facility that includes limited open/visible storage accessible to visitors, a working paleontology laboratory also visible to visitors, work and office space for park and visiting scientists, rangers, and other NPS staff, an auditorium, and a classroom/meeting room. The structure also serves as the park's main visitor center; as such it includes the main information desk staffed by the Interpretive staff, as well as a small sales area managed by the park's cooperating association, the Northwest Interpretive Association, which offers an assortment of books and other related educational materials for visitors to purchase.

The structure includes fire detection, fire suppression, and security systems, which provide a high level of protection based upon the latest technologies available for the collections exhibited and stored inside. The main exhibition gallery, where some exhibits do not have glass tops, but do have alarms responsive both to contact switch disruption or motion, is out of sight of the ranger staffing the information desk. Therefore, security cameras would be a good addition to the overall security system.

Exhibit areas include the main central lobby (which also houses the information desk and sales outlet) where eight stand-alone museum exhibit cases are located. The design of the cases is such that they can easily accommodate temporary, rotating exhibits. Windows into the paleontology lab and collections storage on the west side of the lobby enable visitors to observe the preparator at work preparing fossil specimens and take a peek behind the scenes and see collections storage. Finally, the entryway into the main museum gallery is to the southwest of the lab, towards the building's front entrance. The gallery has a multi-faceted exhibition devoted to the "Age of Mammals" featuring various fossil specimens, interpretive panels, artwork, and other media devoted to the 40 million year time frame represented by the various fossils discovered in the park.

The collections storage, work, and office areas are just as impressive as the exhibition galleries. A 1,600 square foot collections storage area adjacent to both the lab and offices is in addition to the aforementioned paleontology lab. Storage furniture includes several racks of metal shelving, an insulated fire-resistant lateral filing cabinet for museum records, and about 70 full-height museum cabinets, both visible storage cases with glass doors and standard, closed, all-steel doors. The room has a desk/small work area and a computer and workstation with the ANCS+ database, enabling museum cataloging of specimens to occur in close proximity to storage and preparation areas. (See Issue C for additional information concerning museum collections storage at the park.)

As noted in Issue C, collections storage at the Paleontology Center undoubtedly should meet the needs of the park for the next five to ten years, unless the park obtains an overwhelming number of exceedingly large and unusual accessions. As archives will undoubtedly prove to be a major part of future collections growth, an archives survey should be programmed at the earliest opportunity (see Issue B for further details concerning archives and records management).

The other park facility that houses museum collections is the Cant Ranch House, located in the Cant Ranch Historic District. This multi-use facility, which previously served as the park's visitor center prior to construction of the Paleontology Center, still serves a visitor services function; it also houses park administrative offices and storage areas (both museum and administrative files storage).

The first floor contains exhibits related to the area's cultural history. Upon entering the house, the two large rooms to the left contain exhibits pertaining to the wide expanse of the area's human history: the original Native American inhabitants, European explorers, traders, trappers, miners, Anglo settlers, and ranchers. The conflicting ideas, competition, and eventual violence between Indians and American settlers related to land use and differing ideas of "ownership" are also represented. A small room to the right of the front door is historically furnished to the circa 1920s ranching period, and contains numerous artifacts (furniture and small personal items) on loan from descendants of the Cant family. An office used by visitor services staff is also on this floor.

The second floor of the ranch house is devoted to the park's administrative offices: superintendent, Division of Administration, integrated resource manager, and law enforcement. The third floor is currently used as supplementary museum storage for artifacts, herbarium and insects, and potential archives, and for the storage of old administrative files. The space also houses the uninterruptible power supply equipment for the building's computer network.

Storing museum collections in such a mixed-use area does not meet NPS museum standards for security and preservation. Although the majority of the collection is housed within locked storage cabinets, various oversized items such as maps and plans (which potentially are archival materials) are stored in the open in a haphazard way, partially rolled up and contained in a large cardboard box. As such, these items are at risk from damage caused by rodents and other pests as well as being misplaced or lost (all park staff have a key to the third floor space). Fortunately, this area, like the rest of the structure, is equipped with a modern fire detection and suppression system and a relatively new HVAC system, and could be readily retrofitted with barriers. However, in the opinion of the MMP team, this location is not as appropriate as the library in the TCPC for storage of archival collections.

The museum collections are documented by both accession and catalog records. The park maintains these records in the Thomas Condon Paleontology Center. Since the park was established in 1975, the unit has created 355 accessions that document nearly 60,000 specimens and objects. These accessions have been generated through field collections, incoming loans, donations, transfers, and purchases. In the preceding thirty-two years, the staff has generated over 13,000 catalog records that currently reside in the ANCS+ museum catalog database.

Despite the above efforts, there are gaps in the JODA collections' documentation:

- Accessions data in ANCS+ do not always agree with the corresponding catalog data (for example, object and specimen items counts have not been revised consistently).

- Source of accession data in both the accession book and ANCS+ is sometimes incomplete (or in many cases, such information was erroneously entered into ANCS+, resulting in printed forms not containing all necessary information).

- Incoming loans for collections exhibited at the Cant Ranch have not been formally renewed.

- Accession book entries are not uniformly up-to-date or complete to NPS standards.

- Recent accessions lack appropriate documentation such as Accession Receiving Reports, Receipts for Property, and so on.

- Other accession folders contain the proper documentation, but lack required signatures (such as the superintendent's).

- Accession files and ANCS+ accession records are not up-to-date (the latest accessions in the Accession Book have not yet been added to ANCS+ nor have accession folders with required chain of custody and ownership documents been created).

- Several accession book entries are blank, i.e. these accession numbers have not been used.

Discussion

Museum collections record the resources that the park is required to protect. They offer essential information for management decisions, serve as a unique resource for scientific investigators studying the natural and cultural processes that created the lands within the park, and assist interpretive staff in relating information to visitors. Documenting museum collections is essential; it allows both physical and intellectual access to museum collections for management, education, research, and loans.

The building block upon which a unit's museum collection is developed is the Scope of Collection Statement (SOCS). A Scope of Collection Statement is a stand-alone museum planning document that succinctly defines the scope of the unit's museum collection holdings at the present and for the future. The SOCS derives from the legislation establishing the unit, its mission, as well as laws and regulations mandating the preservation of collections. The Scope of Collection Statement is the critical basis for managing museum collections.

The park has a draft Scope of Collection Statement that was developed with the assistance of the former collections manager prior to his transfer in 2005. This activity is one of the most important curatorial projects that the museum staff can undertake—the SOCS sets the tone for the direction that the collection will take. It provides guidance relative to the acquisition and management of those museum objects that contribute directly to the unit's mission, as well as those additional collections that the Service is legally mandated to preserve. When completed in the near future, the Scope of Collection Statement will:

- define the purpose of the museum collection;
- set agreed-upon limits that specify the subject matter, geographical location, and time period to which the collection must relate;
- evolve from legislation and planning documents specific to each unit, and from laws, regulations, and NPS policies governing research and specimen collection conducted within park boundaries;
- state what types of objects will be acquired to fulfill the park's mission; and
- consider collection use and restrictions.

Development of a Scope of Collection Statement is a group effort. To be an effective document, the participation of the major collections generators and users is required. Though the Research staff will undoubtedly take the lead in preparing the SOCS, input from the resource management and interpretive staffs, at a minimum, is necessary for an effective document. Once the SOCS is approved by the superintendent, the Research staff can produce briefing statements for distribution to park staff, partners, and the public which details the park's scope of collection, specifies the object types and quantities needed for the collection to be relevant to the park's mission, and offers a brief explanation as to why certain items are not required. The briefing statement intended for the public should also include information concerning other known institutions' collecting emphasis and contact information, in order to facilitate potential donations of items not needed by the NPS.

Once the Scope of Collection Statement is approved and collections are acquired, all related museum documentation must meet NPS museum standards. Accession and catalog records must be accurate, legible, and unambiguous. The accession records describe the movement of items to and from the collection and document their legal status. The catalog records provide descriptive and location information for museum objects and specimens. These records provide valuable information that identifies the unique and irreplaceable resources associated with the park. Without accurate documentation, this information will be lost. Documentation is a major part of the accountability process for museum collection management. Correspondingly, accurate documentation also is vital for the collection's use for research and educational purposes. Without complete and accurate description, provenance, and other catalog data which quantifies its unique characteristics, an item's potential for research or interpretive use is severely diminished, if not eliminated.

Acquisition and Use of Collections

Various standard operating procedures (SOPs) pertaining to acquisition of, access to, and use of the park's museum collections need to be developed. The park's Museum Collections Access Policies (see Appendix H for a sample) should be updated and revised, and then distributed to all staff. The museum management program must ensure that all park staff, particularly front-line interpretive staff are familiar with these procedures and that printed copies are available at all contact stations and offices for public distribution, as needed.

The park is encouraged to develop a formal park-wide acquisition policy pertaining to the acquisition of all types of specimens and cultural property, including items intended for interpretive use only, i.e. interpretive "props" used during educational programs. The park is *strongly discouraged* from acquiring authentic biological (skeletal, tissue, skins, and so on) materials unless harvested from road-kills, and all appropriate Federal and State permits have been procured and are on file for inspection by the appropriate regulatory agencies. With today's technology, replica skeletal materials that are extremely accurate and affordable are available from many sources. The use of road-kills and replicas ensures that the park does not unwittingly provide material support to unethical suppliers of supposed "scientific specimens." Likewise, any cultural materials acquired by the park for interpretive use should be modern replicas acquired from legitimate vendors, specifically for educational use.

All such educational props, both cultural and natural items, should be inventoried and accounted for on an Educational Prop Inventory maintained by the Division of Interpretation in concert with other park staff. All such items must be marked with a unique inventory control number applied with permanent ink.

Museum Planning

The park needs to complete a number of planning documents in order to provide the proper documentation, protection, preservation of, and access to its museum collections. Such documents can identify deficiencies, state recommended outcomes, and develop both interim and long-term action plans to accomplish these preferred end products. Examples include Museum Security Survey, Museum Fire Protection Survey, Collection Condition Survey, Collection Storage Plan, Museum Emergency Operations Plan (MEOP), Integrated Pest Management (IPM) Plan, and the Museum Preventive Maintenance Plan. Many of these plans can be funded through the Museum Collections Protection and Preservation Program (MCPPP) program described below, although some do not qualify.

- Scope of Collection Statement (SOCS) – No fund source is available for this document. It is generally completed by park staff.

- Collection Condition Survey (CCS) – This is Museum Checklist standard H6. A deficiency/need for a CCS identified on the Museum Checklist can be funded through MCPPP. Conservation treatments cannot be funded from MCPPP, although CRPP-BASE and CCM funds may be used.

- Collection Storage Plan (CSP) – Although all parks do not need such a plan, JODA would benefit from a thorough analysis of the storage needs of all park collections and evaluation of all possible alternatives for storage of all museum collections – both natural and cultural. This is a standard in the Museum Checklist (H7), so it can be funded through MCPPP.

- Museum Emergency Operations Plan (MEOP) – Every park must have a MEOP, which should be a component of the park's overall Emergency Operations Plan. Museum Checklist standard E8 pertains to the MEOP. Preparation and implementation of a MEOP qualifies for MCPPP funding. The park has developed a draft park-wide Emergency Operations Plan (2005), although it does not contain any information relative to museum emergency operations.

- Museum Integrated Pest Management (IPM) Plan – This should be part of the park-wide IPM plan. Museum Checklist standard H8 pertains to the Museum IPM Plan. Preparation and implementation of a Museum IPM Plan qualifies for MCPPP funding and is a necessary first step in the development and implementation of an ongoing museum IPM program.

- The park has developed a park-wide Integrated Pest Management Plan (2006). The plan includes a section on museum pests, although it might be more useful if the plan included photographs and/or drawings of each type of pest commonly found in museum areas. To ensure that the plan is up-to-date, the park is encouraged to provide a thorough review of the plan by IPM and museum IPM specialists. If in need of revision, the park should program for a revised Museum IPM Plan.

- Museum Preventive Maintenance Plan (called a Housekeeping Plan in the Museum Checklist) – This is Museum Checklist Standard H9. Preparation and implementation of a Museum Preventive Maintenance Plan qualifies for MCPPP funding. This park is in great need of this plan in order to develop and implement an appropriate museum housekeeping program for the Paleontology Center and the Cant Ranch House.

- Museum Security Survey and Museum Fire Protection Survey – The park's two main visitor and museum facilities, the Thomas Condon Paleontology Center and the Cant Ranch House, are equipped with fire detection, suppression, and security systems. **The security system in the Cant Ranch House should be extended into the third floor.** At the same time, it is extremely important to ensure that all installed systems are operable and appropriate for the intended use. Are there any needed upgrades or modifications? Is routine inspection, testing, and maintenance (ITM) of all systems consistently carried out according to manufacturers' specifications and the Fire Code? To ensure that all systems are appropriate and maintained in good working order, the park should program for both a security survey and a fire protection survey. These two surveys, conducted either by subject matter expert NPS or contract staff, will assess all museum areas relative to security and fire protection.

Since the park has not conducted a museum security survey or a museum fire protection survey, the park is encouraged to develop a Project Management Information System (PMIS) Project Statement to address these needs as soon as possible. Fire and security surveys for all museum areas are critical requirements, for they identify needs and deficiencies and thereby establish the groundwork upon which these needs are to be addressed. These surveys can be funded through the MCPPP Program. The absence of a security survey is a deficiency (H2) noted on the park's Museum Checklist; the lack of a fire protection survey (H3) also is noted on the park's Museum Checklist.

Museum Funding

Project fund sources available for the museum collection are: Cultural Cyclic Maintenance (CCM); Museum Collections Protection and Preservation Program (MCPPP); Backlog Catalog Program (BACCAT); and Cultural Resource Preservation Program Base (CRPP-BASE). Each year about $100,000 in regional CRPP-BASE funds are set aside for cataloging museum collections (CRPP-MCBC).

Once the park has identified collections in need of cataloging (and has accessioned the items), it then can request funds through BACCAT and CRPP-MCBC to address the need. Likewise, deficiencies identified in the Museum Checklist can be eliminated with funds from MCPPP. Finally, projects that provide preventive conservation or perform suitable treatments on objects themselves can be funded through CCM. To qualify for project funding, an up-to-date PMIS Project Statement is needed for each corresponding proposed project. Competition for project funds can be intense, so it is vital that the park's PMIS Project Statements reflect current needs and provide clear and concise descriptions, justifications, and budget projections to address the question, "Why should this project be funded over some other park's proposal?"

Project funds cannot make up for shortfalls in base funds, but they can be used to address certain types of planning and programming needs, especially short term projects that produce museum plans or address a particular preservation deficiency. The Museum Collection Preservation and Protection Program (MCPPP), Backlog Cataloging Program, and Cultural Resource Preservation Program Base (CRPP-BASE) are just three examples of such fund sources available to JODA. Although the park has utilized Backlog Cataloging and CRPP-BASE funds as needed, the park currently has no PMIS statements devoted to museum preservation and protection issues that are eligible for MCPPP funding.

Although MCPPP-funded projects for FY2008 and FY2009 have already been prioritized, the park is encouraged to develop PMIS project statements to program for the following museum planning initiatives and projects, all of which would qualify for MCPPP and/or CRPP-Base funding:

- Museum Security Survey
- Museum Fire Protection Survey
- Museum Collection Emergency Operations Plan (MEOP)
- Museum Collections Preventive Maintenance Plan (Museum Housekeeping Plan)
- Collection Condition Survey

- Archives Survey (CRPP-Base only)
- Collection Storage Plan (if needed following the Archives Survey)
- Purchase and Install Environmental Monitoring Equipment for All Museum Areas
- Museum Integrated Pest Management Plan (IPM Plan)

Museum Reporting

Museum Checklist. The park's current Checklist for the Preservation and Protection of Museum Collections ("Museum Checklist") has been brought up to date. The Checklist has been updated since the construction of the Thomas Condon Paleontology Center, and now lists the varied spaces.

The Museum Checklist is an important collections management and planning document. It:

- Establishes the standards under which park museum collections are to be maintained and against which a park evaluates itself.
- Documents the preservation of the park museum collections at a particular point in time.
- Determines the funding needed to bring a museum collection to standard.

The Museum Checklist is divided by facility and type, i.e., a structure that holds both exhibit and storage contains two different museum facilities and both need to be assessed separately. It is vital that the park completes and/or updates this document on an annual basis. Museum Collection Preservation and Protection Program (MCPPP) funding is based on the data derived from the Museum Checklist. To be funded through MCPPP, a project must be in response to a deficiency identified on the park's Museum Checklist.

Collection Management Report (CMR). The Collection Management Report is another museum management report that each park must complete and submit each year. The CMR quantifies total collections activity for a given year and includes accessions, deaccessions, cataloging, object types, catalog backlog, use, and a total collection summary.

As with the Museum Checklist, the CMR is used to prioritize and allocate funding to address needs quantified on the CMR; Backlog Catalog Program fund distribution is based on this report. To be eligible for Backlog Cataloging funds, a park must have a catalog backlog on its CMR, so it is critical that the CMR accurately reflects the total park collection, especially with regard to uncataloged backlog.

As noted above, the park's FY2007 CMR reports a catalog backlog of approximately 5,000 items (85% of which are paleontology). The other collections disciplines of biology, geology, history, and archives round out the remaining 15% of the backlog. As a result of cyclic prospecting and periodic field collections, the paleontological research specimen collecting events will continue to keep a small backlog annually. Archival collections however, are almost certainly underestimated; therefore the archival backlog is correspondingly underreported on the 2007 CMR (see Issue B: Archives, for additional information).

The CMR also reports another important element of collections management: access and use. Access and use of collections data are reported in Section D: Use of Collections. According to the FY2006 CMR, the park maintains 19 loans totaling 487 objects; exhibits 1,255 objects at the Thomas Condon Paleontology Center and Cant Ranch House; responded to 305 research requests within the park and 45 outside research requests.

This last element, research requests from within and outside the park, reports research access and use of the collection. Such data to be included in these two fields include: park staff use of museum collections for research (resource management, compliance, interpretive program development, planning initiatives, maintenance activities, and so on); use of the museum collection by faculty and staff from various universities, museums, or other institutions; use of the collection by other outside researchers, paleontologists, other scientists, historians, authors, and the general public. Such use can either be in person (researcher visiting JODA collections) or via distance (telephone, email, facsimile request for information, and JODA staff accesses collection to provide response to researcher). These data are almost certainly under-representative of the true volume of research requests To provide a more accurate representation of the large research use of the collection, the park should be sure to track *all* such uses and provide these data on the park's CMR. Such data can provide additional support for improvements for public access to collections via PMIS Project Statements and future Operations Formulation System (OFS) requests.

Staffing and the Workload Analysis

Staffing. The natural and cultural resources management programs at John Day Fossil Beds National Monument are unique in the Service—the park in effect has two divisions of Resources Management. Unlike some other parks, which have separate natural and cultural programs, the two divisions at JODA each have some element of both. The larger of the two, the Division of Research, most closely approximates other parks' Divisions of Resources Management and Research, as all three staff members are scientists (paleontologists) engaged in research, publishing, and managing the natural resources (fossils) of the park, as well as museum collections management. The park's Resource Division is exactly that, as it deals with both cultural resources (Section 106 Compliance) and natural resources management related to the living biological ecosystems at the park, especially work related to the elimination of exotic plants, habitat restoration, and fire management. Each division provides a vital component of the park's overall management strategy. At the same time, the museum management function is located in the Research Division, a logical choice, as paleontological specimens comprise over 85% of the total museum collection.

Collections Manager Position. Until 2005, the paleontology program included a full-time, permanent collections manager to provide day-to-day oversight of the museum collection. In the two years that the position has remained vacant, critical museum management needs have been unmet.

Unfortunately, as the staff of the division is engaged in numerous research projects and ongoing natural resources management initiatives (primarily paleontological in nature), no one has been able to undertake day-to-day management of the museum collection. If one of these individuals were to assume collections management duties (which constitutes a full-time workload), their own research and natural resources management work would be greatly reduced. As identified in the John Day Fossil Beds National Monument Business Plan (2006), the park's second highest operations and management strategy is devoted to filling the lapsed collections manager position.

Restoring the collections manager position is vital if the park's museum program is to maintain even a minimal level of compliance with Servicewide policies and accepted museum standards. If the vacant collections manager position remains unfilled, basic documentation, preservation, and protection will not be carried out and the park will be unable to provide an appropriate level of access to this important, one-of-a-kind museum collection. Restoring this position is vital if the park's museum program is to maintain even a minimal level of accountability and compliance with Servicewide policies and accepted museum standards. The park may want to explore filling the position initially as a subject to furlough position. Although the possible FY 2008 base increase of $10,000 devoted to exhibit maintenance at the Paleontology Center was never intended to be for staffing support, it is possible that it could provide up to 1/5 of the funding for this position. (Museum housekeeping such as exhibit maintenance would be carried out by the collections manager.)

The collections manager's importance to the park's overall museum management program cannot be overstated. The collections manager will:

- Implement and carry out daily, weekly, monthly, quarterly and annual museum housekeeping duties at the Thomas Condon Paleontology Center and Cant Ranch House.
- Conduct weekly environmental monitoring of temperature and humidity levels in all museum areas.
- Carry out weekly Integrated Pest Monitoring (IPM) in all museum areas.

- Implement a quarterly light monitoring (visible and UV) program for all museum areas.
- Accession, catalog, research, photograph, and otherwise document museum collections.
- Respond to researcher requests (in-park and outside researchers) and assist and supervise researchers accessing collections.
- Review and comment on museum plans and park planning efforts affecting natural and cultural resources management.
- Implement storage upgrades to ensure that all collections are stored appropriately to provide for their proper preservation.
- Carry out the various annual museum reporting requirements: Annual Inventory of Museum Property, Museum Checklist, Collections Management Report, and the Annual Catalog Card Submittal.
- Prepare loan and deaccession paperwork.
- Research, develop, and install rotating temporary museum exhibits at the Paleontology Center, Cant Ranch House, and other area institutions (for example, other agencies' visitor centers, museums, colleges, and libraries).
- Conduct public relations activities concerning JODA museum collections and resource management issues (such as public information requests, technical assistance to partner and stakeholder organizations, public and school programs, and diversity recruitment efforts).

Until the collections manager position is filled, these duties must be assumed by others currently in the division. Recent managerial recognition of the position as critical to the accountability, preservation, and protection of these valuable resources has resulted in a commitment to advertise and fill the position initially as a GS-07, permanent STF Position.

Fossil Preparator Review. Another staffing issue for the Research Division concerns the fossil preparator, an integral part of the paleontology team. Although currently filled at the GS-7 level, it is a highly specialized and complex position which has accrued new demands and responsibilities since it was first established. In addition, because of the nature of this work; the knowledge base essential to effectively carry it out; and the position's critical importance to the park's scientific, interpretive, and resource management goals and objectives; the position description needs to be revised based on current work and perhaps should be a GS-9. The fossil preparator largely works unsupervised and is expected to make decisions and judgments on treatment of specimens, many of them irreplaceable holotypes.

The Workload Analysis. An analysis should be undertaken to determine the complete workload for museum management for the park. This analysis should be completed by the Research staff and peer-reviewed by the Pacific West Region curator. This analysis should be broken down by the following areas:

- Central work elements that are basic requirements and responsibilities for managing the museum program
- Current hours and full-time equivalent positions (currently being expended)
- Additional hours and full-time equivalent needed to meet all basic requirements
- Needed support costs to administer museum program beyond salary requirements. Funds would cover contracting for specialized services, transportation, supplies, and material.

Appendix B includes a suggested workload analysis spreadsheet that has been used for museum planning at other NPS museums. Data in the spreadsheet should be used to support development of the core operations for the park and inform the budget cost projections for the park. It also provides the foundation for developing other museum planning.

Once all of these data are compiled, and given the critical need for a collections manager and a possible upgrade for the preparator, a new base increase request (OFS statement) should be crafted detailing the needs of the museum program.

Recommendations

- Complete a workload analysis for the park's Museum Management Program to assist in establishing staffing and funding needs.
- Develop additional base increase requests to address park museum management operational needs.
- Fill the lapsed collections manager (GS-1016-7/9) position.
- Develop PMIS project statements to program for the following museum planning initiatives and projects:
  - Museum Collection Emergency Operations Plan (MEOP)
  - Collection Storage Plan (CSP) – if needed following the Archives Survey
  - Museum Security Survey
  - Museum Fire Protection Surveys
  - Museum Integrated Pest Management Plan (IPM Plan) (update and add to the museum section of the park's IPM Plan)
  - Museum Collections Preventive Maintenance Plan (Museum Housekeeping Plan)
  - Collection Condition Survey
  - Archives Survey
  - Purchase and Install Environmental Monitoring Equipment for All Museum Areas
  - Implement a Temporary Exhibit Program to Improve Visitor Access and Enjoyment of Museum Collections
  - Develop a Scope of Collection Statement (SOCS) Review Committee (composed of the chief of Research, Research staff, chief of Interpretation, lead interpreter, chief of Resources, and other interested parties) to assess the draft 2004 Scope of Collection Statement and make recommendations for any needed revisions and additions in order that the SOCS remain supportive of the park's themes and research, interpretive, and resource management goals and objectives. Following these Scope of Collection Statement update scoping sessions, complete and approve the Scope of Collection Statement.
- Reconcile all collections documentation issues.

- Determine legal ownership of collections, especially the items on loan to the park from the late Lillian Mascall.

- Resolve discrepancies in the ANCS+ accessions database related to item counts and types.

- Initiate a systematic review of all accession records to ensure that each accession possesses all NPS chain of custody documents and that all are completed and signed by the necessary parties (recent accessions lack proper documentation).

- Initiate a thorough review of all ANCS+ catalog records to determine which records do not meet cataloging standards relative to identification, descriptive, provenance, and other unique distinguishing and relational data.

- In consultation with the Chief of Interpretation and the Law Enforcement Ranger, develop the following standard operating procedures (SOPs):

    - Opening and Closing Procedures (with a checklist for staff) for the Thomas Condon Paleontology Center

    - SOP concerning staff response to alarms within the Paleontology Center: gallery alarms (1st priority); door alarms

- Develop collections access policies, which balance preservation and access; distribute to all park and partner staffs.

- Program for, purchase required equipment, and implement an environmental monitoring program for all museum areas.

- In consultation with park staff, define how the collections should be used and enjoyed by the public in all formats (exhibits, websites, etc.).

- Develop a rotating, temporary exhibit program in the Cant Ranch House to replace the Lillian Mascall Collection should those items be reclaimed by the Estate of Mrs. Mascall's late son.

- Encourage staff to reference collections in their interpretive programs, public presentations, meetings, and talks in the form of posters, web sites, and visitor contacts.

- On at least a semi-annual basis, Research staff should systematically peruse the Job Hazard Announcements (JHAs) binder to ensure that it is up-to-date and includes all potentially hazardous materials used in paleontology and museum work. The park's safety officer can be of assistance in these efforts. (The Research Division has a binder of JHAs in the paleontology lab and in the Research office.)

- Develop an SOP for borrowed type specimens. Type specimens on loan to the park should be given the highest levels of security and care; they also should be the first specimens to be evacuated in an emergency.

- Continue to ensure that researchers working under permit in the park understand their responsibilities/deliverables related to curation of any specimens or artifacts recovered from park lands, including, but not limited to, cataloging, repository storage according to NPS and accepted museum standards, and providing the park with copies of field notes, photographs, reports, and other associated project documentation for inclusion within the park's archives.

- Continue to provide support for enhancements for the museum management program related to the use of volunteers and Friends groups.

- As needed, develop Repository Agreements with other institutions to house the park's collections of archaeological or other materials for which storage at the park may not be the best option for research access, use, and/or preservation.

Issue B—
Information Management

Issue Statement

Improvement of systems to manage and safeguard paper, audio-visual and digital information resources under the care of the museum and throughout the park will increase their preservation, access and use.

Background

Park Records and Archives

The current management of the museum and archival collections for John Day Fossil Beds NM has been assigned to the paleontological curator and his staff, following the loss of their collections manager two years ago. As the primary resource of the park, paleontological and geological research dominates the activities surrounding the creation of information in the park. The park's paleontological staff and associated researchers have been extremely active for over twenty years recording locality information, creating data while preparing fossil and geological materials, and populating the library with a robust collection of scientific literature.

The scientific staff, in addition to creating ANCS+ catalog records, have developed numerous methodical recording systems and data sets in various software programs that fit the needs of their discipline and document their activities. These data sets are actively and carefully managed and record critical scientific information and comparison data that add significantly, as a whole, to the body of knowledge in this field. However, the loss of the collections management position has deferred duties such as environmental monitoring and processing of collections other than paleontology, particularly the accessioning of any new park records and archives.

The museum holdings also include administrative, interpretive and cultural history records created and assembled in process of the designation of the Cant Ranch Historic District, its preservation and interpretation. Currently, five cataloged manuscript boxes of assembled archives in the collection comprise an important but very incomplete record of administrative history since the park's designation in 1975. In the absence of a collections manager, photographs, drawings and plans, oral history recordings and other materials have been set aside in museum storage, but not yet cataloged into the collection, properly housed or made intellectually accessible. In 2006, the ANCS+ Collections Management Report classified only 1% of over 50,000 items in the park collection as archives, while about 95% are paleontological and geological specimens. While the cataloged archival materials currently in the collection reflect the collecting emphases above, they do not accurately represent the range and quantity of archival materials which are lingering unidentified in museum storage, various offices, closets and cabinets throughout the park.

Permanent park records cataloged as archival materials in the museum collection preserve and make accessible the history of activities and management of the park unit as a whole. At the outset of the MMP team's visit, the unit superintendent expressed his concern and priority to better identify, organize, and more easily access park records. In turn, creating a better understanding by park staff of accountability during active records management, both paper and digital, improves access and long term preservation of information resources when they enter archival status. Records status is determined by their classification in *DO#19, NPS Records Disposition Schedule*. Once these resources are accessioned into the museum collection, they become the responsibility of the museum program whether or not they are transferred to a Federal Records Center or stored in the park collections. To achieve control over and access to active and archival records in the park, the museum program must expand and manage the scope of materials needing to be included in the park archives.

While most divisions and programs now report or store data electronically in NPS database systems on the intranet, parallel paper and other media records were and are generated by all offices. The information contained in park administrative and resource project and management records, correspondence (including email), audio-visual materials, maps, plans and drawings, photographs, reference materials, digital data sets and images play a key role in documenting park resources, recording park history, supporting current park operations, and preparing for future information needs. As of 2006, NPS required each employee to complete an online records management training course hosted at www.doilearn.gov. In the park survey, however, only the keeper of the central files and the park ranger/historian had a ready copy of *DO #19* to classify records and understand which were permanent. Her copy was the 1986 version, which has since been updated.

During the MMP team site visit, a preliminary survey was conducted to identify potential paper, audio-visual, and digital record groups throughout the park offices. The results of the survey (see Appendix D) for physical materials, indicate that over 4,410 individual items, 90 linear feet of boxed materials and 350 plans, maps, and drawings need review by an experienced NPS collections or records manager and/or an archivist to determine their disposition, whether that be inclusion in the archives, the library, or scheduled for destruction. If even half the surveyed material were to be accessioned into the collection, 76,760 items would be added, far exceeding, just in that discipline, the total number of all currently cataloged collections (50,323 items) combined.

It will be necessary to plan for the growth and management of the archives collection and strategize about climate controlled centralized storage and access for a minimum of 60 linear feet of records, audio-visual storage, and flat files. The June 2004 Scope of Collection Statement (SOCS), states that administrative and resource records throughout the park classified as permanent should be sent to the Federal Records Center. While this is an option, for various reasons the records of resource management and administrative activities of a unit are now believed in most cases to be more useful and accessible when managed by the park.

However, in the absence of the collections manager position being filled and no archivist on staff, the park will need to prioritize committing resources toward reaching the desired goal in conjunction with project funds available from the NPS for archival surveys, processing, and cataloging archival materials. Much of the work of establishing an archive fully representative of the park is out of the realm of the current staff's professional expertise. The creation of archival collections and finding aids is specific to the training of archival science. Whether in a printed copy or searchable electronic format, the production of finding aids when cataloging archival collections is the key to providing every staff member equal and easily understandable access to the document and image collections.

A survey presented to the park in advance of the team's visit showed seven out of ten respondents as regular users of the library and museum collections. Only two people reported using the present archives collection. In comparison to the more well developed and cataloged resources, the low number points to both lack of archival materials in the collection and access to them. In addition, the park interpreter/historian reported that she receives requests for historic photos throughout the year and uses the uncataloged collection to fill them.

Digital Information Resources

The JODA staff is following the trend of most other parks in amassing digital photos without a system or software program to manage them and their associated information. This is a concern to the museum program, for many of these images are park records and eventually will need to be added to the archives. The chief of Interpretation reported having several thousand digital images in their division. The Facility Maintenance Division has documented projects digitally for 10 years. All of the image files are stored on a computer or a network drive with minimal organization or identification. The paleontology program keeps a number of digital data sets, including photos of every specimen drawer, over 150 .pdf files of research papers and a digital collection of field photos referenced by number in their field notebooks. These photos are originally digital and therefore have no paper equivalents to manage as they are printed only when needed for reports, brochures, signs and so on. Each division expressed a serious concern over how to manage, organize, and backup these resources.

Another critical issue is the lack of written identification stored with the images—the who, what, when, where, and why. As the images age and staff leaves, the task of identification becomes time consuming and overwhelming. The information not recorded may be lost, and at best is recoverable by spending more valuable resources.

The data sets of the paleontology program are primarily electronic information resources, not all in NPS supported software, and are sometimes based on or converted from hard copy original sources, such as field notes, correspondence, and bibliographic citations. The stability, security, and accessibility of these data sets and how they will survive and migrate into the future are of concern to the museum staff. As records of museum activity and collective knowledge, they are currently in an active status and are managed as such. But as they age, they may be converted or consolidated or outlive their original purpose and become inactive, eventually suited for scientific and historical research of a different nature.

The paleontology program has scanned and created digital data from original paper or film materials, including aerial photos and slides. It is important to recognize that digitization of original documents is not the same as preservation. Digitization is often essential for ease of access, but there is no NPS or other standard for securing the longevity of digital information. The security of sensitive information, such as locality data, must also be considered. Computer hard drives crash, disks corrupt, backups can be irregular, people start and don't complete digital projects, reformatting becomes expensive as hardware and software advances, and storage mediums change. In only 15 years the industry has taken us through several sizes of floppy disks, zip disks, CDs, DVDs, external hard drives, memory sticks, and file format standards. However, in the discussion section there are suggestions for gaining control and organizing these resources, until such time as parks are provided more software or web-based systems supported by NPS.

ANCS+ Archives Records

Archival entries in ANCS+ require special attention to reflect accurately the quantity of archives in a collection. A review of JODA accession and catalog records in ANCS+ concerning archival material revealed the records need to be corrected and standardized. There are inconsistencies in properly categorizing and counting archives. Many accession records mistakenly categorized archives as history objects. Also, the quantification of archives is different from counting objects and requires consistency in entering item counts or linear feet to achieve the most accurate count. For example, JODA 4516, Administrative History Records, is entered in the accession record as "5 history (bulk) items and 1 archival item (estimate)." In the catalog record the collection is quantified as "5 boxes of archives."

These entries are inconsistent and skew the numbers in the annual Collections Management Report (CMR). The totals in nearly all the accession, catalog, and the backlog records of archival materials are inaccurate and need to be adjusted. The project should be undertaken by a collections manager or archivist with the advisement of Kathleen Byrne at the National Catalog as to any requirements for documentation to account for the differences in changes in older accession records and recataloged records. Changes made to these records will appear in the CMR at the end of a reporting year.

In addition, an unexplained drop by nearly 2/3 of the archives cataloged occurred between the 2004 and 2006 CMRs from a total cataloged of 1,457 to 529. No recorded deaccession accounts for this change. A correction of the accession and catalog records may reveal the reason for the change in numbers, but an issue of accountability is pending until the museum can account for this change.

Storage

The paleontology staff stores archival information and specimens related to their disciplines in their office complex at TCPC. The biology, cultural, and most of the archival materials in the collection are stored on the 3rd floor of the Cant Ranch House. Issue C of this plan on preservation discusses in more detail the competing uses of the area (heating, IT server, records storage), and addresses issues of security, environmental monitoring, and pest control. The 3rd floor contains photographs, historic documents, and park records stored there pending accessioning and cataloging, and cartons of administrative records awaiting their retention period. Oversize plans and maps are temporarily stored in the room, rolled and laid flat on tables and open shelving. Fifteen drawers of flat files are empty, likely due to an inventory of the materials in process. However, their temporary storage in short boxes and piled on tables are detrimental to the items, leaving them vulnerable to light, pests and damage. An attempt should be made to carefully organize and store them on the open flat shelving or in the drawers while the inventory is proceeding.

There are some problems with the current storage of archives related to creating an optimal acid free environment that can be readily corrected. These are addressed in the Discussion section of Issue C in more detail.

Paper and audio-visual materials are particularly sensitive to high temperatures and humidity. Monitoring will help to determine what measures might be taken to achieve a consistent range of < 74 degrees F and < 70% relative humidity. In combination, conditions regularly exceeding these levels can stretch, shrink, and tighten audio and video tape, and separate layers and chemical binders on photographs and film. Paper is subject to mold and fungus growth, book lice, and pest damage from silverfish and other cellulose eaters.

Figure 5 Cant Ranch House 3rd floor permanent collection storage Room where temporary records are also stored.

Evidence of the presence of past visits of dermestid beetles and rodents was found on the 3rd floor. In addition, pests and molds can be inadvertently introduced to the collection area when records boxes and materials from other buildings are moved into it. If another location cannot be found, the purchase of a chest freezer is recommended to treat incoming records from the park and donations from the outside before they are stored in the same room. Security is also an issue for stored records which contain sensitive information such as travel, payroll, and personnel. They are accessible to anyone with the common key to the area. Until they can be secured or relocated they should be taped securely shut and monitored for tampering.

Library

The park library consists of over 12,000 reprints of scientific literature cataloged in Endnote, a bibliographic database. With the assistance of Nancy Hori at the Regional Office, about 3,000 books have also been cataloged in Voyager, the NPS web-based library catalog. With the move to the TCPC, the library is well organized. A security gate has been installed to protect rare books and the valuable reprint collections of Paleontologists Shotwell, Whistler, and White. A large collection of other collected reprints is in the main library along with books, periodicals, reference materials, park reports, and oral history transcripts.

One staff member in the Interpretation Division, who is also the park historian and in a Library Studies Graduate Program, has been assigned collateral duty for the library. However, only 10% of her time is allotted for this purpose. The library has long depended upon several dedicated volunteers working with the paleontology curator to accomplish its goals. The park may want to consider a professional librarian or library internship as another way to optimize work planned and done with the library resources.

While the Endnote software program serves the needs of the paleontology program, others feel that access to library materials using the Endnote database is a hindrance. This should be alleviated by training staff in the uses of the application. A full set of park reports and plans for reference is also missing in the library. The library does have room for growth and the paleontology staff should consider whether any other large reprint collections may be important to acquire in the future.

Oral History

The park has an informal oral history program that dates back to the 1970s, when interviews with the ranching families and others were taped on cassettes. About 90 cassettes exist; perhaps half of the tapes have been transcribed and none are cataloged into the museum collection. Currently, when time allows or an opportunity presents itself, the historian uses a digital recorder to conduct interviews.

Discussion

Establishing and Managing Archival Collections

The park management has expressed a desire to move toward more active park records management and the establishment of an accessible park archive. First, the language of the SOCS should be changed to reflect the inclusion of permanent administrative and resource management records from throughout the park into the museum archives.

Many aspects of planning and working toward this goal would benefit by the assistance of a professional NPS archivist. The park might consider an archivist-of-record agreement with another park in the Network or Region, committing resources for at least 2 to 3 pay periods a year to bring an archivist to the park on a detail. Or, for the vacant collections manager position, a person with a records or archival management background in addition to science should be considered.

Using the Preliminary Survey in Appendix D as a guide, a PMIS funding request to CRPP Base should be submitted to conduct a thorough survey, accession the park records, and relocate the records to an appropriate area for processing. The accession should use the estimate of linear feet based on the number of boxes assembled until the collection is processed. A second component of the request should be for BACCAT or CRPP-MCBC and would cover the cataloging, re-housing, and creation of finding aids to the collections. This project should figure in the salary equivalent to a GS-09 or above professional series archivist for the project.

The park may want to discuss the idea of combining, in the future, the library and archives collections into the current library space at TCPC.

With the addition of compact shelving and a new storage plan, the library space could hold twice the amount now stored. Request for compact shelving for collections can be made in a PMIS statement to MCPPP or to Cultural Cyclic Maintenance. The gated area could be reconfigured to hold archives if the entire area with shelving now were replaced with compactor aisles. Several rows holding archives could be locked to protect the archival materials. The locked shelving system for protected materials and open library rows has worked well at Hawaii Volcanoes National Park Library in a room of comparable size. Present shelving could be placed on the compactor carriages, making the system much less costly. A long table could be set up in the entry to accommodate researchers and a similar computer station as now, for the librarian and researchers cataloging and accessing databases. Moving the archives to the library would mean a consolidation of all paper, photos, tapes, videos, CDs, DVDs and perhaps oversize documents, creating improved security, storage, environmental controls, and access. The park management, museum, and Library Management Committee should discuss this idea in more detail.

A secondary plan for storing the new archives would be to purchase proper cabinets or shelving or, if adequate, repurpose the shelving holding temporary records on the 3rd floor of the Cant Ranch collection storage. A minimum of 60 linear feet should be planned for the park records collection. Paleontology records listed in the survey also need to be appraised for inclusion in the archives. They should remain in the paleontology offices as controlled property if access is needed more than three times a year or they have associated materials which are still active.

The paleontology program has created access to all the cataloged archives in the collection on an item level in a software program called Idealist. There are 1,172 records in Idealist, a software program no longer supported. The park plans to convert these for use with Microsoft Access when the collection manager position is filled. This system has met the needs of the Department thus far, but as the archives grow it is neither practical nor sustainable to individually enter information about each item. Nor does the rest of the park have ready access to it. Rather, best archival practices rely on the creation of a finding aid to describe hierarchical record groups, their creators, scope, and content and on the arrangement of the records, both intellectually and physically, to retain order and relationship.

The preliminary records survey indicates that approximately 8,000 slides, 3,000 prints, 50-100 videos and 86 audio cassettes in Interpretation, Paleontology, Resources Management, and Facility Management offices need review for inclusion in the collections. Fortunately, most are very well labeled for easier cataloging. All of these resources will need proper storage boxes and arrangements to make their subject matter accessible for research. Again, a qualified archivist can determine from the materials the best approaches to these arrangements.

Another issue of concern is the protection of paleontology locality data when providing qualified researchers with sensitive data necessary to their research. If locality data is published, information about that locality is no longer protected from a Freedom of Information Act (FOIA) request. Managers of NPS collections can set written policy for collections use by which researchers must abide. If it is necessary to share sensitive information, the museum will run a risk, so should have the researcher sign a declaration of use outlining the restrictions, which may include peer review by the park of any material to be published. The museum may want to consult with the solicitor for a formal opinion on this matter particularly as to any precedents or prosecutions for researchers disregarding the policies.

Records Management

While the activities of the park focus on paleontological collections that grow with research and collecting, all divisions generate potential park archives, as the park's activities are managed on an annual cycle. The park unit must commit and cooperate to develop and implement various components of an information management program(s). This should include various park-developed data systems incorporating NPS policies that concern the management of park records: *DO#19: Records Management; DO#25: NPS Museum Collections Management; DO#28:*

Cultural Resource Management; and NPS-77: Natural Resource Management.

Developing such a program will help to eliminate the loss of vital park information and baseline data. Ideally, all park divisions should work together to develop policies and procedures that could be shared and implemented. For instance, a policy on records management (which would assist in identifying permanent resource management records) is essential. This would allow for a formal program which could dovetail with archives management and systematically identify and transfer records to the park's museum collection. Such a policy should include the participation of both a records manager and the park staff that is responsible for managing museum collections.

Appendices E, F, and G—respectively NPS Records Management, Preparing Inactive Records for Transfer to Storage, and Archiving Resource Management Records to Museum Archives—provide instructions and forms which can be adapted for use by all the park divisions for guidance on creating a park system for records. The JODA museum program has developed a library of Standard Operating Procedures (SOP). These cover many aspects of museum management, computers, correspondence, field work, GIS, operations, and other aspects of controlling and organizing information. The Appendices in this report should be added as guidance the museum can use and provide to park staff for records management. The role of individuals as their own record managers is augmented by required online training and assistance initiated by a collections manager or an archivist. Their role is making the final appraisal of the record sets using *NPS DO#19, Records Disposition Schedule,* and to determine permanent retention of all park records. The schedule can be accessed through the inside.nps.gov home page. Through a link on InsideNPS a .pdf of the schedule is available. All park staff can benefit by additional records management training, but as keepers of the central files and administrative records, the administrative staff should be provided opportunity to attend a thorough training course provided by NPS or DOI.

Facility Management and the superintendent are cooperating on a plan to organize and duplicate a working set of the plans, drawings, and maps found in the park. While this puts the archives one step ahead, they should be sure to work with the museum to return all originals to the archive for accessioning and cataloging. There are no cost or low cost duplication services for these items at the Technical Information Center (TIC) at the Denver Service Center as well as scanning services. All scanned items are put in the TIC database so both the visual item and its description can be searched and retrieved on the website. For questions or requests, TIC can be contacted at TIC-requests@nps.gov, or called directly at 303.969.2130.

Digital records present additional challenges and steps for identification and preservation. The park, as it moves toward more native digital resources, would benefit by forming an Information Management committee. The group should include the persons responsible for IT, and representatives for the Museum/Library, Interpretation, Facilities and Resources. The issues discussed in the following paragraphs would be among those on an agenda of attempting to plan for and manage digital information as a whole. Server capacity, backup, storage needs, consolidation or conversion to web based data storage, and electronic records management policy and practice are all integral to managing electronic records for the long term. This is one area where individuals should not operate in a vacuum, but plan together for their network needs and operations. Digital information storage and preservation is a complex topic, rapidly changing and not yet well managed by the Service at the park level. Therefore each park should begin to identify their own needs and unresolved issues and contact various IT, program, and resources heads throughout the NPS and inform them of these needs.

It is important to begin to coordinate the management of GIS information with that of an archive management program and to submit metadata records to the NPS Clearinghouse for geospatial data. The website www.fgdc.gov is a gateway to the information about the data standards, access, and warehousing of dynamic ESRI information sets. In the museum alone, more than ten active in-house databases document all museum activities and information. These data are on a server array backed up regularly as well as on a laptop computer which is stored offsite each evening.

In the absence of an NPS supported software program, some parks have successfully adopted Filemaker Pro, Extensis Portfolio, or Thumbs Plus, three long-running proprietary software programs, for managing digital libraries of images and documents. The single application software costs about $300-500 and the server versions of these programs are in the thousands of dollars. However, they can be an indispensable tool for organizing and storing all park images, .pdfs, and digital documents. Their ability to carry descriptive text information in the same record as the image prevents loss of image contents and allows keywords and full text searching to retrieve images as well. With almost 100,000 images now on the JODA park servers, such a tool might be a valuable investment for the organization, future use, and access of these digital resources.

The FOCUS NPS Digital Library can also be accessed through the main menu at the inside.nps.gov home page. Staff should take the simple online training course for FOCUS on doilearn.gov. Once completed, a password can be requested from the FOCUS program manager to post digital images (single or batch uploads) and documents on the NPS site or the public side of the website. Images can now be uploaded to PMIS to illustrate projects if posted on FOCUS. While not an in-house management tool, FOCUS is a very stable place to upload and share information. The paleobotanist's .pdf files would be well placed here. An extended search can retrieve documents and images with associated information from across databases and websites in the NPS and outside repositories.

The museum program should also consider uploading the Endnotes database of paleontological literature to NPS NatureBib database for a wider sharing of materials, or entering the information into the Voyager database, the NPS library catalog. Either web application will provide access to a wider audience.

Email is another prolific digital information resource through which the majority of park correspondence is now conducted. All employees need to be aware that NPS email which each employee creates containing substantial discussion of administrative and resource management issues is official correspondence and should be printed out and filed. Any email written and sent through nps.gov can be subject to subpoena in a court of law.

Preservation

A number of rare books in the park library need conservation treatment. A PMIS statement with a request for Cultural Cyclic Maintenance funds will pay for a book conservator to prepare a Treatment Report with a plan and quote to perform the necessary repairs. Book conservators might be located by contacting Harpers Ferry Center, Pacific Northwest Paper Conservation Services in Seattle, or UC Berkeley Conservation Lab.

Currently the administrative archives collection is arranged by year, which gives no descriptive clues to its content as a whole. When the rest of the administrative records are processed, a comparison should be made with the cataloged collection to see where the current records fit in and possibly rearrange or recatalog them with the rest of the collection. At a minimum the cataloged collection needs rehousing. Clippings and fragile materials are stored without protection among the other documents. Files and storage boxes should also be better labeled with accession and catalog numbers, date ranges, and box sequences (1 of 2 etc.).

All oversize items stored in flat files (paleontology and 3rd floor collections) should be placed in uniform non-buffered acid-free map folders. The park's photo collection of negatives and prints (over 2,000 items) all need to be rehoused in acid-free sleeves and envelopes. Slides should be stored in poly sleeves and binders. Aerial photos need rehousing in acid free sleeves, folders, and boxes. Other photographic and historic documents in the collections also need to be housed and stored properly.

The exhibit on the first floor parlor of items on loan contains original framed photographs and certificates archival in nature. If they are to remain on exhibit, their condition should be examined by an archivist and paper conservator. If they are deteriorating they should be returned or facsimiles should be made and exhibited and originals stored before irreversible damage occurs.

For preservation purposes the rare and fragile Shotwell collection of reprints in the library should be taken out of shelf files and stored horizontally in file folders inside labeled manuscript boxes in the library. Shelf file storage and access is damaging the materials. A handful of very rare books in the library should also be identified and cataloged into the museum collection. They should be non-circulating and can be stored in the library with their location information in ANCS+.

About 80 original oral history recordings on tape are stored in the Cant House in Collections Cabinet 1 and in the historian's office. Transcripts and files on the interviews should all be correlated and organized. All of the material should be accessioned and cataloged into the museum collection for preservation and accountability of this primary resource. The cassettes were recorded in the 1970s-1980s and due to age, they are a priority for examination by an archivist for condition and possible reformatting. The Interpretation Division has an interest in capturing more interviews, but this effort is not fully developed or recognized as a process that also involves steps to preserve and make accessible the information. The museum program would benefit by working with Interpretation to ensure the materials are preserved and made accessible by assisting with a plan. Developing such a plan would result in an interview list of not only local history figures, but key figures in the community and the service who were involved with the development and management of the park, such as the park's first superintendent and the first NPS paleontologist.

Recommendations

- Adjust the SOCS to reflect the inclusion of permanent administrative and resource management records from throughout the park in the museum archives.
- Pursue the assistance of an archivist-of-record to assist with planning, ANCS+ records clean-up, and project management. Secure project funds to provide professional archival planning and oversight of archival projects associated with the Museum Program.

- Correct past accession and catalog records to accurately classify and quantify the archives in the collection. Review the classification process for new accessions and catalog records.

- Use Appendices E-G to inform administration and all staff of a systematic approach for reviewing and submitting permanent records and reference materials into the archives and library on a regular schedule.

- Improve digital information management by forming a park-wide committee to address digital information issues and solutions.

- Prioritize reformatting and proper storage of documents, oversize materials, and multi-media for preservation and access.

- Consider the future relocation and consolidation of archival museum materials to the library at TCPC for management and improved access, or revamping of 3rd floor in Cant Ranch House.

- Using finding aids, image software, FOCUS, Voyager, and NatureBib, provide enhanced intellectual access to staff and other collection users of bibliographic information, images, and archival documents.

- Include the museum program in planning for oral history to include time and personnel for the transcription and cataloging of tapes, digital recordings, and transferal into the museum collection along with background information and an index to recorded subject matter. Accession oral history media into the collection and request funding for cataloging and transcriptions.

- Make archival training courses and records management courses available for staff.

- Due to their condition, rarity, and value, rehouse the Shotwell collection of library reprints according to archival standards.

- Create PMIS funding request for CRPP Base to complete an archives survey and accession park records into ANCS+. Add a component for BACCAT or CRPP-MCBC funding to process and catalog park administrative history records, using preliminary inventory in Appendix D for an estimate.

- Create PMIS request for rare book conservation.

- Consider skills and background in cultural resources, archives and library, as well as natural resources when recruiting a collections manager.

Figure 6 Truck in field behind Cant Ranch Barn showing adaptation as a crane; not a museum item, 2007

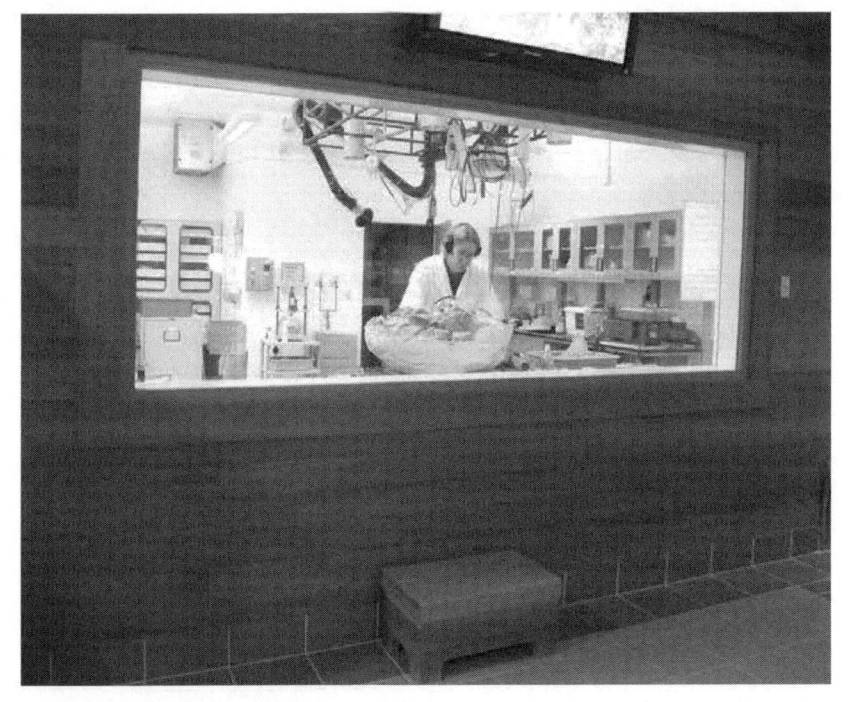

Figure 7 Preparator Matt Smith in paleontology lab on view to visitors in Thomas Condon Paleontology Center, 2007

Issue C — Collections Preservation

Issue Statement:

Developing collections assessment and monitoring protocols and analyzing storage needs and potential upgrades will result in a better use of available resources to enhance effective collections growth, use, and protection at all levels.

Background

John Day Fossil Beds National Monument has been known to the world-wide paleontological community since the 1870s for the depth and range of its spectacular fossil resources. Though the monument was not founded until 1974-5, fossils were scientifically collected and maintained in several major collections before that time. JODA was established by enacting legislation specifically to protect the fossil resources on the designated National Park Service lands. There are three main separate units in JODA: Clarno Unit, Painted Hills Unit, and Sheep Rock Unit. Other federal and state land management agencies protect associated lands, most notably the Bureau of Land Management (BLM) and the U. S. Forest Service (USFS) on the 10,000 square miles of potentially fossiliferous lands, some under interagency agreements with JODA.

JODA's research and collections emphasis is on Cenozoic fossils, particularly vertebrate faunas and all floras in a continuous record from 45 to 5 million years ago. Over 2,000 species of plants and animals have been identified from JODA, including some of the earliest and most notable specimens collected.

In 2004, NPS opened the Thomas Condon Paleontology Center (TCPC) at JODA as a combined visitor center and collections and research center. The exhibition galleries opened in 2005. Since TCPC opened, visitation to the park has increased roughly 6% each year. The most recent visitor counts are 27,000 visitors to the TCPC in 2003 and approximately

125,000 to JODA lands overall. A third of the TCPC visitors also go to the Cant House across the road, the park's historical interpretation and administrative center. The Central Oregon region is a center of population growth, concentrated in the Bend area two and a half hours to the west; visitation is projected to continue increasing. JODA is a non-fee park, so income from the TCPC derives primarily from the bookstore and donations.

Collections are at the core of JODA and TCPC activities. Although research, collections, and other programs are not specifically mandated in the omnibus enabling legislation, it is not possible to analyze, understand, and protect fossil resources without a strong program in collections and research. Fossils are a non-renewable resource and must be collected and preserved in order to be studied, identified, and interpreted. This creates the need for good collections care, including good storage, documentation, and handling and access policies and procedures.

Over 90% of JODA object and specimen collections are paleontological, as is most of the park research. This section of the report does not include detailed concerns with archival, photographic, documentary, and reference collections at JODA, since those are being addressed separately. The remaining collections are recent biological specimens, historic and cultural holdings, and archival resources. BLM archaeologists in Prineville generally oversee JODA ad hoc archaeological surveys, and any resulting collections are managed by NPS archaeologists and stored at other NPS sites. There is some evidence that archaeological resources on JODA lands are more significant than thought or anticipated by many, and that a full-scale archaeological research and collections program could overwhelm JODA resources. Since there is no JODA archaeologist or program, partnering with BLM and other NPS units on this issue appears to be a good working solution. In return, JODA, under interagency agreements, acts as the repository for fossils in its time range collected on four BLM units and three USFS units.

The paleontological collections storage and work areas at TCPC are excellent. The storage cases are presently not of the compactor type. This is a viable option, given the floor strength and case layout, and one that will need to be explored in the future as the collections grow. JODA collections will remain at the park with room for another three to five years of collections growth at the present rate without adding new cases or compactors. With growth projection for another 20 years, however, it is obvious that both the number of cases and their efficient arrangement will be critically necessary to make the best use of the available space.

Collections are also stored on the third floor of the Cant House, an area with several conservation problems in terms of pest access, security, and visible and ultraviolet light exposure. This area houses historic, cultural, and art objects, archival materials, and a few biological collections. A detailed conservation and collections management survey of this area should be conducted with an eye toward partitioning this area and removing collections that are more appropriately stored at the TCPC or in outside repositories.

JODA manages an active program in recording non-native and rare plants on its lands under its natural resource management program. Plants have been identified and inventoried since 1977, and the first wildlife inventory was completed in 2004. The current project of inventorying plant specimens includes voucher specimens which will be added to the museum collection.

Discussion
Collections Management Issues

JODA currently operates with no collections manager, a position previously dedicated to care and management of the paleontological holdings in the TCPC. This has resulted in a loss of primary management of collections transactions and baseline environmental monitoring activities. There has never been a program of dedicated collections management for the biological and historic/cultural holdings at JODA, or for indoor integrated pest management. While the overall environmental conditions and storage systems at TCPC are new and of good to excellent quality, conditions and storage systems at the Cant House are problematic and need monitoring and documentation. In addition, a program of environmental monitoring needs to accompany a program of inspection and housekeeping in the exhibition areas at both facilities, including the agricultural machinery kept outdoors on the Cant House and barn grounds. A good environmental monitoring program for the collections and exhibits at JODA will require a dedicated collections management position.

Environmental Monitoring

JODA is located in a relatively mild climate in eastern Oregon, in the rain shadow of the Cascades. This region is much drier than the Pacific Coast region, but somewhat more temperate than the Plains states to the east. A review of 50 years of climate data shows that temperatures rarely go above 90° F or below 20°F, though spikes of 110°F and –24°F have been recorded. A weather station is located just outside the TCPC building and is checked and recorded regularly as part of the natural resources program. Precipitation rarely ranges above 2" in a month, though there have been high rainfalls above 4" in the spring months and high snowfalls in December and January. There can be little to no precipitation in the summer months. High temperature (T) and relative humidity (RH) levels have not been a problem in the TCPC since it opened, given the monitoring records that exist. There are no comparable records for the Cant House, which is less well equipped with building environmental systems.

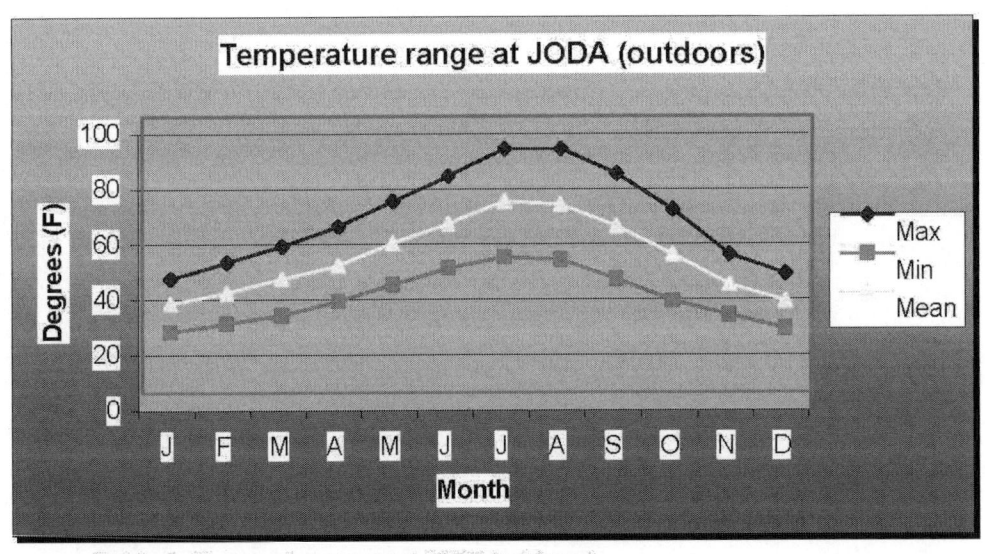

Table 1 Temperature range at JODA (outdoors)

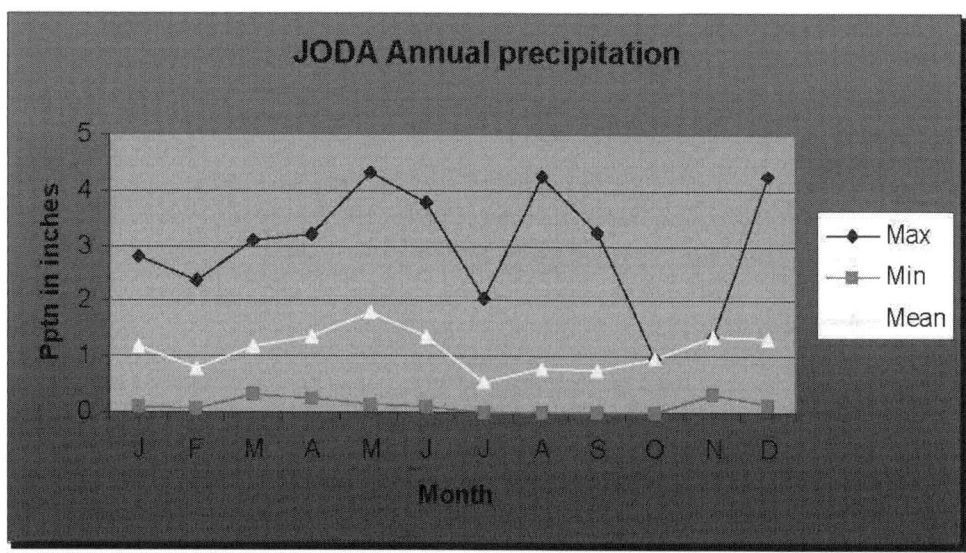

Table 2 JODA annual precipitation

There has been a program of monitoring internal temperature and relative humidity levels at the TCPC via data loggers, but much of this work has been discontinued with the loss of the collection manager position. It needs to be revived and expanded. As a primary NPS collections center and a Federal repository, JODA needs to provide good collections care, which includes good environmental conditions within the building at all times. Comparable environmental monitoring needs to be initiated in the Cant House on its first and third floors.

No climate control protection can be made for agricultural implements and machinery stored outdoors on the grounds of the Cant House and its barn. Serious reconsideration of this strategy is necessary, as the implements are visibly deteriorating, a practice that does not reflect well on JODA or the NPS. At a minimum, they should be moved into the barn if they are of any value to JODA at all.

Temperature

Most of the collections at the TCPC are paleontological (original specimens and casts) and library/archival holdings. The original fossil specimens are relatively resistant to damage caused by temperature spikes and fluctuations, though some adhesives and consolidants (and possibly some cast materials) may be damaged by extremes. Charts from data loggers showed that temperatures stayed in a conservationally comfortable range of 68-75°F with the building heating, ventilating, and air conditioning (HVAC) systems turned on. The park has developed an aggressive energy management plan for the TCPC to save energy. The HVAC system stays on 24 hours a day, seven days a week. The temperatures in collection storage and the library are controlled by separate fan coils that operate constantly and never shut down. The set points on the other fan coils are changed when the building is unoccupied or at the end of the day through the use of unoccupied set points for temperature. Collections storage and library set points are not changed between occupied and unoccupied set points. There does appear to be a problem with excessive humidity fluctuations which needs to be investigated. HVAC systems are maintained for the care and safety of collections as well as for human comfort, and collections care does not stop at the end of the workday or on holidays.

Relative Humidity (RH)

No adverse RH readings were noted in the data logger records that exist for the paleontological collections. These readings were noted in the 45-60% range. Again, while the original fossil and cast specimens per se are relatively unaffected by RH extremes and fluctuations, the clay minerals in geological matrix material are wildly susceptible to any RH changes. Library and archival materials are also sensitive to high and low RH conditions, as are organic materials in the holdings at the Cant House (such as wood, hide and skins, biological specimens). There is no evidence that the TCPC RH has ever reached 70% or above, the level at which mold and mildew can start. It is not known what the RH is at the Cant House for any of its areas. The HVAC systems need to be kept on to keep RH levels as stable as possible, generally at 50% or below for both buildings.

Data Loggers

For both temperature and RH concerns, the program of monitoring internal conditions using downloadable data loggers needs to be revived and expanded to cover a wider range of areas, including microclimates in both JODA buildings. All collections, including the library and exhibition areas, need to have data loggers in ceiling, floor, and internal case placements, for a minimum of three per room. These should be downloaded monthly and posted on an internal staff website for reference.

JODA may want to consider a system of radiotelemetric data loggers that will download information automatically and remotely. These are more expensive but would facilitate checking and recording all data logger information in both buildings.

If conditions in the Cant House third floor are not in the appropriate range for good care and conservation, the use of this space for collections storage should be seriously re-thought. As noted in Issue A, a storage evaluation and plan needs to be completed which would review all alternatives for storage of all museum collections and make a proposal based on the long-term preservation, protection, and accessibility of all the collections.

Light and UV

There is good ambient light in the collections, exhibition, and work areas of the TCPC, with no external windows. External windows are provided in TCPC offices and are present on all floors of the Cant House. Clerestory windows illuminate the main atrium of the TCPC. The TCPC collections and laboratory areas that are visible to the public are necessarily kept illuminated during normal visitation hours, but are otherwise turned off when the areas are not in use.

No amount of ultraviolet radiation is desirable; all sources of UV should be blocked. UV radiation is a primary contributor to the yellowing, embrittlement, fading, and physical breakdown of many museum materials, including all organic materials and specimens, archival holdings and certain adhesives and consolidants. The TCPC and the Cant House should be completely UV-free in all interior areas.

The major sources of UV radiation in interior areas are unfiltered fluorescent fixtures and unfiltered windows and skylights receiving solar illumination. The amount of current UV radiation can be assessed with a UV meter. All windows and skylights should be protected with UV-blocking film, and all fluorescent fixtures should be equipped with UV-filter sleeves. These are available from several conservation and archival suppliers and are good for several years after installation. UV readings should be made at least annually after films and filters are installed to determine when these are beginning to fail and in need of replacement.

Light and UV Meters

The JODA collections management program should invest in good light and UV monitoring equipment for assessing ambient light levels and the efficacy of UV filtering materials. These readings should be made monthly for at least the first year to establish a baseline of annual ranges of ambient light.

Integrated Pest Management Indoors: Monitoring, Response, and Control

Overall, the TCPC and the Cant House have low levels of museum pests. Entomological collections on the third floor of the Cant House have been attacked by dermestids in the past, and there is concern about rodent harborage in JODA buildings. Incidental pests noted on this visit include bats (as evidenced by feces) in closet areas on the third floor of the Cant House, various insects on windowsills also of the third floor of the Cant House, and sphecid wasps noted in light fixtures in the TCPC.

The paleontological collections have not attracted any primary museum pests, and JODA does not provide any food or beverage concessions. There is a staff conference/lunchroom that should be kept clean. Food and drink are not allowed in collections areas. A good coordinated pest monitoring program will provide a baseline for assessing the presence of and response to primary and incidental pests in the TCPC and Cant House facilities.

Pest Monitoring

Monitoring pest presence should begin with a coordinated program of placing, reading, and recording pest presence in passive traps. These traps are not a means of pest control and should not be viewed as such. Key areas for floor-level sticky trap pest monitoring include all areas in which collections are stored in the TCPC and Cant House, all gallery and interpretive areas, areas in which food is stored and consumed by the staff, and areas in which pest presence has already been noted (entomological cases and the third floor of the Cant House). Key areas for flying pest traps include unobtrusive areas inside the TCPC.

No primary museum pests have been noted at the TCPC. Sphecid wasps pose no direct threat to collections of any kind, although the dead wasps are an available food source for more problematic species such as dermestids. Other than monitoring to establish baseline numbers, no particular measures are indicated within the TCPC at the time. All areas in which collections supplies, especially cardboard and paper, are stored should be carefully monitored to check for signs of insect infestation. All doors to the outside should be kept closed, and any incoming biological materials should be bagged and isolated for at least two weeks to check for any signs of pest infestation.

The Cant House poses more problems than the TCPC; it is an older structure with more pest-attractive holdings and areas. Special attention needs to be given to the windows and eaves with regard to blocking insect and bat entry points. Many species of bats are protected at both the federal and state levels, so eradication is not an option; however, the bat droppings are both a pest food source and a potential threat to human health (respiratory concerns). Bat experts can advise on a legal and effective strategy for blocking all entry points at a time and in a way that will not adversely affect the survival of the animals. Both closet areas will need a thorough professional cleaning to remove the feces.

All the windows of the Cant House likewise need to be surveyed and caulked or blocked as necessary to prevent insect and other pest entry. In addition, a thorough survey for the presence of rodents in both buildings should be undertaken. While a few mice may be inadvertently caught in sticky traps, the best approach is a blacklight survey of key areas to detect rodent urine traces. The Cant House in particular is vulnerable to rodent attack. One exhibit, a sack of sheared wool, needs to be monitored on a daily basis. It is an excellent rodent harborage, and no pest control methods can change that. If any evidence of pests is discovered during the monitoring, then the park will need to evaluate its options: removal of the exhibit or replacement of the contaminated material. Indoor rodents, particularly wild mice of the *Peromyscus* species, can pose a primary human health hazard through exposure to viruses shed in feces and urine. The storage cabinets in the Cant House containing biological specimens should also be monitored, with traps both inside and outside the cabinets.

All traps should be checked regularly, at least monthly during the spring and summer months, and notes made on the identity and frequency of any trapped species. Software for mapping trap results across the building areas over time is available from several sources. This will aid in fine-tuning any necessary response strategies.

Pest Response and Control

No chemical methods of pest control should ever be used within the TCPC or the Cant House; both are public buildings with steady public visitors and permanent staff offices. Insect infestations should be controlled insofar as possible by isolation, freezing, and improvement of the affected case and area before the collections are returned. If there are serious concerns with indoor rodents, extermination needs to be handled by NPS professionals experienced in IPM methods approved for use in public buildings.

Physical Cleaning and Housekeeping of Exhibitions

Part of the collections management work at JODA should be the regular inspection and cleaning of specimens and objects on exhibit at TCPC and the Cant House. A quick check of specimen and vitrine surfaces in the TCPC exhibitions area revealed slight amounts of dust and at least one spider web strand. NPS has published guidelines for cleaning vitrine surfaces and furniture materials, appropriate for guiding a program of exhibition conservation at the Cant House, but the fossil specimens in open-topped cases must be dealt with carefully by someone with a good knowledge of the composition, sensitivity, and importance of the specimens and their associated information. No cleaning fluids or sprays should ever be used on fossil specimens, whether originals or casts. The discussion to obtain a conservation-grade vacuum with appropriate filter attachments should be revived in light of the conservation needs of the TCPC gallery. Inspections of TCPC exhibition areas should be done at least monthly by a collections manager or paleontology staff member to check for misplacement, damage, or loss in addition to cleaning needs.

Other than the program of conservation and monitoring mentioned above, JODA needs to develop, in conjunction with a dedicated collection management program, a good program of preventive gallery conservation for both TCPC and the Cant House. This would include the development of an inspection checklist (in conjunction with a good security survey) and a cleaning protocol and schedule. Conservation vacuuming and dry dusting, condition checks, and a cyclic maintenance program need to be under JODA collections management requirements. Cyclic maintenance and an annual deep cleaning should be included as well.

Inspections of the Cant House exhibits should be done on a parallel schedule by a collections manager familiar with the needs of historic and prop objects in interpretive exhibitions. Baseline levels of current fading and other damage should be recorded for future reference.

The outdoor agricultural implements should be documented in their present condition to establish a baseline against which future deterioration can be measured. There is no point in expending park resources to conserve these objects if their storage situation is not responsibly improved. If they are not critical to the active interpretation program at JODA, they should be transferred to a facility able to maintain them under best practices and standards for the care of historic machinery. If they are critical to the interpretive program, then they should be entered onto the park property inventory and managed as such.

TCPC Collections Storage

Collections storage at JODA can be grouped into three main areas: the primary paleontological, exhibition, and library collections areas at TCPC; the exhibitions and third floor of the Cant House; and the grounds of the Cant House barn. The TCPC paleontological collections constitute over 90% of JODA holdings and are the most rapidly growing.

Paleontology Storage Analysis

The largest collection, as noted, is the paleontology collection, numbering some 55,000 specimens. These include original specimens collected on-site since 1975 as well as casts of pre-1975 specimens made from originals in collections held in other research institutions, notably the University of California - Berkeley, University of Florida, and University of Oregon. Some comparative osteology specimens are also included, but there is not yet a comparative herbarium. However, with the relatively new paleobotany position and the need for comparison of fossil and living plants, this is one area of the collection that is anticipated to grow. JODA is particularly strong in vertebrate paleontology and in paleobotany, and most of the future collections growth, both fossil and comparative specimens, is projected along those lines. In addition, JODA serves as a repository for contemporaneous specimens collected in other Federal land units (BLM and USFS) in the region. On-site management of JODA fossil collections is of core importance to the park's mission; retention of the collection as NPS property is mandated the 1906 Antiquities Act.

Although the enabling legislation mandated the naming of the park's principle visitor center after Thomas Condon (TCPC), 25 years elapsed between the enactment of the legislation and the securing of funds to build the center. TCPC is designed to serve as the fossil collections center for JODA in perpetuity. It is possible that another 20 feet of space could be obtained by extending the collections area of the building, but no one sees this as likely. All analysis and projections, therefore, are based on the assumption that the amount of space currently available for the paleontology collections and research program will be constant.

While a detailed collections conservation survey has yet to be done, it is worth noting that there are few of the classic fossil conservation problems (pyrite/marcasite deterioration, Byne's "disease" of calcium carbonate structures, and gypsum/anhydrite problems). The most vulnerable geological materials are the clay minerals found in the various strata. The worst damage recorded in storage cases is a past dermestid attack of pinned entomological specimens stored on the third floor of the Cant House.

Paleontology: Cabinetry

All paleontology and comparative osteology collections are stored in good-quality steel cases with good gaskets and closures. There are no substandard storage cabinets. These include standard museum cases, tall half-unit cases, visible storage cabinets with inset windows, and a few non-standard units that are equivalent to standard specimen cabinets. Standard quarter units are preferred for the expansion of the paleobotany collection, while the tall and narrow half-units are preferred for the remainder of the collections. Some open shelving for oversized materials is available; this uses particle board for shelving, which could be upgraded to steel but is not a primary concern. All cases are currently standing directly on the floor, without case risers.

JODA vertebrate fossils range in size from tiny single mammal teeth to very large skulls and post-cranial elements. Plant fossils range from microscopic palynomorphs to large petrified tree trunks. The ongoing program of fieldwork and casting of specimens on loan results in a net increase to the vertebrate holdings of three half-unit cases every year. The addition of a staff paleobotanist has resulted in a fast-growing and well-researched paleobotany collection that has the potential to grow at the rate of one standard museum cabinet every year with recent comparative specimens included. Space needs to be calculated for the separation of composite assemblages into separate specimens and for the addition of administrative orphaned collections.

There is sufficient space to add another bank of cases (two rows back-to-back) without compactorization, as the aisles are quite wide,[2] but the park should ensure sufficient floor-loading capacity and stability to permit future compactorization. The cases now have about 20% capacity for more specimens. At the current rate of growth, another bank of cases will be necessary in five years; compactorization will be necessary in ten years. This rate could be hastened by the addition of administratively orphaned or private bequeathed collections from several regional small colleges, museums, and collectors. Space for these should be factored into the long-term storage plan. All banks of cases should be cabinet sanitary platforms

---

[2] Concern was expressed that aisles between cases have to be wide enough to permit full-turn wheelchair access under provisions of the Americans with Disabilities Act (ADA). This is not required at all. As long as the aisles are wide enough (48") to allow case drawers to be pulled out completely and safely, and work areas and finding aids are fully ADA compliant, the aisles can be made considerably narrower.

until such time as they are compactorized, in order to facilitate cleaning and prevent pest harborage.

A quick assessment of the main collections area showed that the main purchase need at this time is more standard museum cabinets for the paleobotany collection. These cases can be stacked two- or even three-high against one wall and can remain as a fixed aisle in compactorization. This would free up a number of the tall and narrow half-units for the faunal collections with no additional purchase. Oversized shelving can be moved to the opposite wall and can also be left as a fixed aisle. Non-collections items should not be stored in or on top of collections cases, and equipment supplies for collections should be stored separately, perhaps in the laboratory area.

Cases in the accessions area room could be arranged and filled to better maximize the available space; cases could also be added here without the need for compactorization. The cases with windows are excellent for display in the areas with windows into the public area. These should be monitored with the case screen open and closed in order to determine how the open screens affect internal environmental conditions.

Use of Collections

Access

TCPC collections are reasonably accessible, though work areas need to be evaluated under a collections/lab access plan for sufficient space, finding aids, and other accommodations. There is, appropriately, no access to the collections area without a member of the paleontology staff with a key card, so most access issues can be facilitated through staff assistance. Given the current issues with fossil market values, it is not appropriate to leave any visitor unescorted in the collections or lab areas.

The collections at the Cant House are not accessible under ADA guidelines, but they are accessible to anyone who is physically able to ascend the staircase and has a key to the door. Park staff on the second floor do provide some monitoring of who is accessing the space. Security restrictions as noted elsewhere in this report need to be put into place for any JODA collections that will remain in the Cant House. Overall, however, this is not an adequate collections space and cannot be made accessible even with handrails.

All exhibition areas in TCPC and the Cant House are accessible in terms of physical access and good line of sight. The TCPC exhibition area in particular is well-designed for just this purpose. Future exhibit enhancements at both the TCPC and Cant House might include hands-on casts and Braille or other text accommodations for sight-impaired patrons. In either case, all public facilities and services are to be accessible to the public, as is reasonable in expense and in keeping with resource protection. Park staff needs to ensure consultation occurs with the park accessibility coordinator on any new exhibits or programs.

Outgoing and Incoming Loans

TCPC manages an active loan program, mainly to receive and prepare casts of fossils from the region collected before the park was created. A member of the paleontology staff manages this program and the resulting cast specimens are integrated into the TCPC paleontological collections.

Molds/Casts

JODA manages an active molding and casting program in order to obtain a good representative sample of fossils collected prior to the creation of the park. In return, JODA provides and receives casts of fossils under an open exchange program with several institutions. This has created a good reference collection supporting research both at and of JODA resources. The casts are treated as specimens and are integrated into the collections.

Out-gassing Molds and Casts

In a few cases in the TCPC vertebrate fossil range, some casts are giving off a noticeable odor most apparent when a case door is opened. This indicates that certain casts are off-gassing and are most likely continuing to react and deteriorate over time. It would be very useful to target these casts to determine their origin and, if possible, the nature of the casting material.

Because these casts may well be deteriorating, their use in morphometric analyses may be compromised as their dimensions change, especially in small mammal tooth specimens. It is recommended that TCPC isolate these in passive oxygen-barrier film enclosures, though it is not necessary to create an anoxic environment within the barrier film enclosures. The off-gassing vapors may otherwise affect other storage materials in closed cases.

Notes on Public Programs and Interpretive Collections

The interpretive programs at TCPC use a variety of hands-on specimens, mostly reproductions, in a series of educational programs focused on the JODA fossil biota and the methods and materials used in modern paleontology. This is an excellent program and is currently expanding and developing. One cautionary note here: if modern biological specimens are to be used for comparative purposes, as is most appropriate, care must be taken to obtain these legally and with full state and Federal permits as required. It is possible to purchase osteological specimens from unscrupulous dealers without permits, and this could cause serious trouble with U. S. Fish and Wildlife Service. A better strategy would be to use durable casts from legally collected specimens in museum collections.

Storage Materials and Repository Standards

As called for in the standards NPS requires of its repositories, TCPC is itself a repository that meets or exceeds most of the criteria NPS has set. JODA is not accredited by the American Association of Museums, in common with most NPS units, but may wish to evaluate the costs and benefits of AAM accreditation as part of a long-term strategy.

Particular storage standards that JODA meets as a fossil repository include:

- All flammable liquids are kept away from the area where the collection and documentation are archived.
- Drinking, smoking, and eating do not occur in the storage area.
- The storage area for the collection is separate from offices and preparation labs and has few doors and no windows.
- All fossils are stored in a stable condition, kept in ethafoam-lined boxes within drawers

- Each fossil is kept from rolling
- TCPC uses acid-free paper and boxes to house fossils and documentation.

Cant House
First Floor

The first floor of the Cant House is dedicated to exhibits interpreting the ranching history of the area in general and the Cant and Mascall families in particular. There are concerns with these exhibits from conservation and legal issues. The JODA administration needs to review these issues objectively and come up with an updated interpretive and historic furnishings plan that takes these issues into account. These areas need to be overseen by a collections manager.

On the left side of the main door as one enters are two rooms furnished with a series of wall and floor vitrines, featuring objects and interpretation of the human history of the area from prehistoric times to present. A number of objects, including a teacup and the seashells in the frontier cavalry exhibit, are cataloged JODA items, and there are reproductions of items associated with the family including photographs and documents. The remainder have been purchased with JODA funds as exhibit items. While these are legally owned by JODA, care should be taken in all records to document the fact that they are not park-specific associated objects, but under current NPS museum policy they need to be accessioned and cataloged. They should be under a regular program of inspection and conservation by someone with collections management expertise to ensure their stability and integrity.

A parlor room on the right side is furnished with objects originally provided on loan from Lillian Cant Mascall. This loan was not renewed before Mrs. Mascall's death and was void upon her death; these objects have now reverted to her estate, and any further loan must be renegotiated with the estate representatives. It is possible that they will be removed.

Without approval from the legal owners, JODA should not directly restore or conserve any objects in this room until and unless a new agreement is reached. In the meantime, however, JODA is obliged to continue inspections and monitoring of these objects, and is liable for damages. The future use of this room should be reviewed under the provisions of a historic furnishings plan, which JODA needs to develop as a top priority. Perhaps refocus the room to interpret the story associated with the ranch which may exemplify one of the ranching stories of central Oregon. However, the Cants' role in the bigger picture is extremely appropriate, as James Cant was a successful rancher and an acknowledged leader in the community when the ranch was at its height. The interpretation of this story is a key component in providing valuable connections to the surrounding community. A collections manager can be tasked with registration functions such as managing loans and renewals needed for this. The park's Interpretion Division needs to take ownership of this story.

Third Floor

The third floor of the Cant House is a multi-purpose storage area including a fan coil unit, an uninterrupted power source, administrative archives, building and exhibit plans, cultural and biological collections, and archival photographs, papers, and sound recordings. The archival issues are dealt with in a separate section of this report.

The third floor area has not been monitored for environmental conditions in some time. There is some HVAC control of the space, and most of the collections are in acceptable to good steel storage cases. There is no access control or motion sensing system, however, and the area can only be reached by a wooden staircase without handrails. Fire extinguishers are placed on the floor, not in holders. The third floor is not a work area and should not be treated as such. Overall, any collections stored here should be removed to a work area on the second floor of the Cant House or to the TCPC for study and analysis.

The windows on the third floor are double-paned, and all have dead insects on the sill between the panes. These should be checked and better sealed. All windows and fluorescent fixtures need to be filtered for UV emissions. As noted, bats need to be blocked from entering the closet areas, and bat droppings need to be professionally removed. This is a human health hazard.

There is no coherent arrangement on the third floor, and anyone with any need to be up there has access to everything stored there. Collections uses and security and maintenance uses are incompatible. It is highly recommended that some form of partitioning be installed so that collections objects in storage are not accessible to anyone who is on the third floor with no need to access collections. Permanent JODA archival materials should be transferred to the TCPC library area.

There are two cases of historic and cultural materials that need to be reviewed and surveyed for their condition, conservation needs, association to JODA, and historical importance. Many of these are organic in nature (wood, leather) and are also subject to pest attack. These will require good security provisions (partitioning, locked cases) and regular pest and environmental monitoring. Art sketches, building designs, and paintings are stored in several cases and need to be transferred to the flat file available on the floor; these should not be stored with other types of materials or specimens. It may be desirable to transfer these to the TCPC library with the archival holdings.

Recent biological holdings need to be carefully reviewed; most are neither accessioned nor cataloged. These materials need to be evaluated to determine whether they should become part of the museum collection. Plant voucher specimens are very important to have as comparative materials when identifying native versus non-native species and identifying rare species. The recent collection of moths may also be of value. Fewer than 3% of total JODA holdings represent biological materials outside the TCPC comparative osteology collections. There have been discussions of moving the entomology collections to Oregon State University and the few mammal skins to the Burke Museum but this decision should be made in concert with the integrated resource managers needs. As the insects have suffered from dermestid damage already, this may be the best course of action. Some aquatic invertebrates are stored in vials in ethanol; these should also be moved to another facility. The relatively small herbarium is also stored on the third floor.

Historic Outdoors Exhibits

By far the biggest concerns are the Cant House barn and agricultural implements surrounding it. As has been noted earlier, the Cant Ranch Historic District is on the National Register of Historic Places and the farm equipment is mentioned in the nomination. The preservation of historic objects in the environment is problematic and creates a heavier workload than maintaining collections in a building. There is even concern about the objects located inside the barn. The barn is a historic structure with a recently replaced roof, but it has a dirt floor and is completely open to the external climate conditions. Lambing pens (jugs) are located inside, and shearing sheds outside. Some historic objects are inside, and on the grounds are several large agricultural implements and machines as well as a badly deteriorated automobile. A cache of search and rescue equipment is also maintained in the barn. Notably, Maintenance and Interpretation Divisions also use this space for storage of non-museum materials.

JODA administration needs to evaluate the best uses of these holdings in light of NPS and professional museum standards for responsible care and conservation. The farm machinery still outside could be moved inside the barn once a determination has been made in consultation with the ranching community about which ones are important to the story, which ones have a reasonable life expectancy under cover, and which ones should be disposed of. Museum objects should not be displayed out of doors but less significant machinery could be if it is managed as park property.

Method	US $	Quantity Needed
Relative humidity indicator card	2-5 (package)	Good to use in all areas for a quick backup check
Thermometer	2-5	Data loggers are better investments
Electronic monitor	30-100	
Mechanical psychrometer	65-100	
Electrical psychrometer	150-300	
Thermohygrometer	800-2500	
Data logger	100-250	~20 for TCPC and Cant House total, not counting units already in operation
Light meter	125-1000	1
UV meter	125-5000	1

Table 3 Cost estimates for common environmental monitoring supplies

Recommendations

- The program of monitoring internal conditions using downloadable data loggers needs to be revived and expanded to cover a wider range of areas, including microclimates in both JODA buildings.

- If conditions in the Cant House third floor are not in the appropriate range for good care and conservation, the use of this space for collections storage should be seriously re-thought.

- Purchase good light and UV monitoring equipment for assessing ambient light levels and the efficacy of UV filtering materials.

- All the windows of the Cant House need to be surveyed and caulked or blocked as necessary to prevent insect and other pest entry.

- Complete a thorough survey for the presence of rodents in both buildings should be undertaken. Check traps regularly, at least monthly during the spring and summer months, and notes made on the identity and frequency of any trapped species.

- Produce a Preventive Museum Maintenance plan and implement a good program of preventive gallery conservation for both TCPC and the Cant House. Cyclic maintenance and an annual deep cleaning should be included as well.

- Document the outdoor agricultural implements in their present condition to establish a baseline against which future deterioration can be measured.

- Assess agricultural implements to determine if they are critical to the active interpretation program at JODA. If not, they should be transferred to a facility able to maintain them under best practices and standards for the care of historic machinery.

- Purchase additional standard museum cabinets for the paleobotany collection which can be stacked against one wall.

- Reorganize storage to accommodate additional storage and move oversized shelving to the opposite wall.

- Program for an historic furnishings plan or other interpretive planning for exhibits in the Cant Ranch House.

- Reorganize Cant Ranch House third floor space to provide for additional security and proper access for the collections stored there.
- Transfer archival materials to another, more appropriate, location such as the library area of the TCPC.

Issue D — Collections Development

Issue Statement

Growth of the collections and their subsequent curation, organization, and maintenance should reflect the park's mission and serve to complement and support the park's research, resource management and interpretive programs. Following formalized procedures will ensure the highest level of care of the collections, associated data, and documentation.

Background

The collections of JODA include paleontology, geology, biology, archeology, history, and archives (See Table below). Unregulated growth of the collections can place a strain on limited park resources in terms of staffing, materials and supplies, and space. Consequently, the park's active research program must consider both immediate and long-term impact to the park's collections since the science of paleontology is intrinsically collection based. Collections development is concerned not only with the quantity of specimens housed in the park museum and the rate at which they are acquired, but also the diversity of materials housed and the curation needs of different types of collections. These relate to various environment and storage requirements, and how the materials will support the park's research, interpretive, education, and exhibit programs.

The predominant component of the park collections is paleontology; this will continue to be the primary area of growth. As might be expected, the related discipline of geology is the second most active. While biology, history, and archeology are all represented by the park collections, they are only minor components and growth has been minimal. The collections do not include any ethnographic items and objects related to this discipline are not likely to be included in the future. Planning for collection growth is critical for the park obtaining funding needed to provide the staffing, equipment, materials, supplies, and space to properly provide for the long-term care of the specimens. The current number of cataloged items in each discipline is listed below.

Discipline	Cataloged	Not Cataloged	Totals
Archeology	4848	0	4848
Ethnology	0	0	0
History	1,520	41	1,561
Archives	3517	12	3529
Biology	533	9	542
Paleontology	41154	4050	45,204
Geology	2428	586	3014
Totals	**54,000**	**4,686**	**58,686**

Table 4 Number of JODA cataloged items in each discipline

While growth of the park collections is ultimately determined by the Scope of Collection Statement (SOCS) as at other parks, at JODA the SOCS is complemented by the park's Paleontological Research Plan (PRP) which dates to 1989. The PRP directly impacts growth of the park collection as it identifies the types of research projects the park will pursue. In turn, this research directly determines the types and quantity of specimens that may be collected. The PRP should be reviewed, accomplishments evaluated, and potential new projects identified. While all potential projects identified in the PRP may not result in the collection of specimens, they all will generate data which may be represented by field notes, maps, stratigraphic sections, and photographs. Each project at a minimum generates items that will eventually be placed in the park archives and will require the expenditure of time and money on its organization and storage.

The Paleontology Research Plan therefore has a major impact on park budget, space, and equipment requirements of the museum collections and staffing, both permanent and seasonal. Each project in the PRP should include a projection as to whether it will generate specimens for inclusion in the park collections or records for the park archives. Each project's scope, objective, product, methods, staff, and benefits and potential for generating museum collections should also be identified. This will help ensure that costs of preparation, cataloging, and curation are included in the budget for the project.

The SOCS as of 2004 identifies the basic mission of JODA to facilitate paleontological research and education in the John Day Region. Therefore, all fossils collected from formations in the park or are directly related to the geological formations found in the park are considered to be within JODA's appropriate scope of collections. JODA is the lead partner in paleontological research and resource management on federally administered lands in Eastern Oregon and has ongoing cooperative agreements and MOUs with other agencies such as the Bureau of Land Management (BLM) and Forest Service (FS).

As part of these agreements, in addition to the field collection of specimens, JODA provides preparation and curation of all specimens recovered, which also contributes to the active growth of the park's collections. This cooperation between agencies is highly commendable and should be continued. It does, however, increase the rate at which the collections will grow and it contributes to staffing needs, space demands, and the costs of collection care at the park. The park benefits from the relationship with other agencies in multiple ways, such as the BLM conducting archeological surveys for compliance. More critical to the issue of collection growth is funding provided for collection care by these agencies, specifically the BLM. This has clearly demonstrated the value of this partnership in not only contributing to the growth of the collections but their maintenance as well.

Overall workload for the museum is not just acquisition and cataloging. For paleontology, a critical element of collections development is the preparation of the fossil specimens and removal of the rock matrix. This work is probably the most time-consuming.

Discussion

Collection Components

Paleontology

Paleontology comprises 90% of the museum collections at JODA. This has been the area of most active collection growth and will continue to be the discipline that will contribute to the growth of the park's collections. Currently, the major portion of the park's paleontology collections is vertebrate fossils.

While traditionally the primary emphasis has been on fossil vertebrates, the addition of a paleobotanist to the park staff will increase the rate at which fossil plant material is added to the collection. While preparation of fossil plants may not require the same amount of time as vertebrates, plant specimens can be considered equivalent to fossil vertebrates with regard to time required for cataloging and space requirements (except for pollen and phytoliths) in the collection. All park documents should recognize this component of the paleontology program and include the term flora whenever the term fauna is used. In addition to vertebrate and plant body fossils, park paleontological resources include invertebrate body fossils and trace fossils such as tracks, burrows and coprolites. These specimens provide important paleoecological information but will remain a small part of the collection.

An average of 3,000 new cataloged paleontology specimens were added to the park's collections each year from 2000 to 2006. While it is not possible to predict the size of specimens collected as they can range from as small as an individual rodent tooth to large elephant bones, a reasonable estimate of space requirements is that on an average, 40 specimens properly housed can fit into a drawer. This translates into 75 drawers, which would fill three of the style of cabinets used for fossil vertebrates each year. The current estimate is that an active paleobotany field project will fill one standard museum cabinet per year.

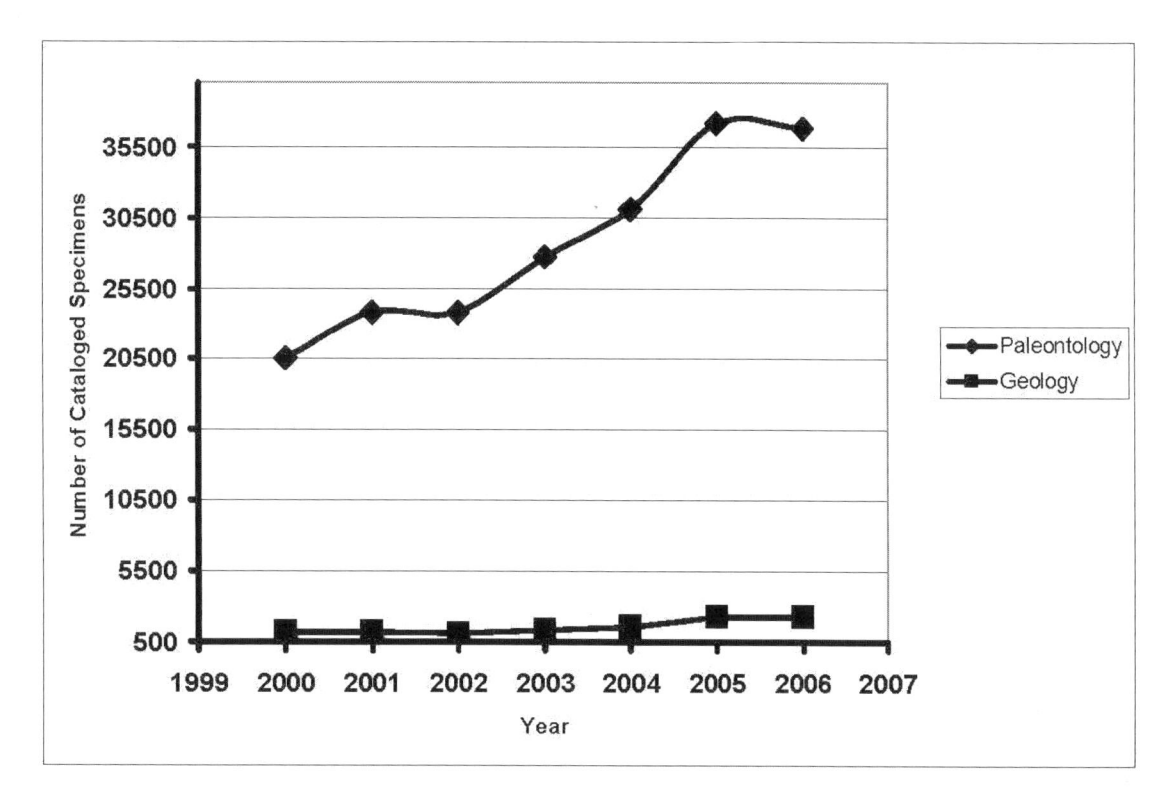

Table 5 Number of cataloged paleontological and geological specimens in JODA collections from 2000 to 2006 based on park-submitted CMR

Another area of collection growth is the active program of borrowing John Day specimens in other institutions that were collected prior to the establishment of the park for the purpose of molding and casting. These historical specimens, particularly types, as well as casts of other outstanding examples of JODA fossils housed in outside repositories, support not only the research program as important reference specimens, but casts of these specimens can also contribute to the exhibit and interpretive programs of the park. The park has made molds and casts of 155 holotypes of vertebrates from JODA. These represent approximately three-quarters of the known described holotypes.

Collection growth will also result from the park's active open exchange program with other institutions for casts of specimens. Unlike the collection of original specimens which is open-ended, the molding and casting of historical specimens has a finite project life and eventually its contribution to collection growth will be minimal. As an observation, given the sensitive nature of borrowed specimens, particularly holotypes, extra care should be given to their storage in locked cases while they are at the park. They should also be stored in such a way that they are quickly accessible for evacuation during an emergency and are addressed in the museum component of Emergency Operation Plans.

As part of the paleobotanical research program the paleobotanist intends to acquire digital images of fossil plants for reference. These specimen images will not be included in the park collections per se but should be handled as a data management issue.

Geology

Although the number of geology specimens is considerably smaller than paleontology, this is the second most active area of collection growth (see Table 5). Voucher specimens of different sediments related to studies of paleosols and tuffs, and for petrographic analysis of sediments resulting from research projects related to paleoenvironmental reconstruction, radiometric dating, preparation of zeolitized and silicified matrices, volcanic histories, geomorphic studies, rates of deposition, diagenesis, and paleomagnetic polarity will be added to the collection. Most of these are hand samples and are of small size. They will require minimal preparation, and the time required for cataloging and curation is no greater than for fossil specimens.

Biology

Comparative Collections (recent osteology, recent plants/leaves)

The park maintains a collection of skeletons of modern vertebrates as a reference collection. Specimens in this collection may not only be derived from the park but will also include exotic species obtained from zoos and other sources outside the park. Data associated with any specimens obtained from a zoo should include the Integrated Taxonomic Information System (ITIS) number, veterinary medical history, and necropsy results.

The park has prepared a list of taxa from about 50 families of vertebrates that would be useful as comparative specimens. This list should be updated and attached as an appendix to the SOCS to serve as a guide as to the taxa to be acquired. Acquisition of these specimens will be over an extended period of time so while they will increase the collections, this aspect of growth is finite and will cease once the requisite specimens have been acquired. All modern osteology specimens should be accessioned and cataloged. The park has indicated that in order to maximize the use of the modern skeletons for reference they would be arranged as a synoptic collection by bone. In order to ensure that the separated bones of a single individual can be re-associated, each bone should be identified with a park catalog number. All specimens should be completely degreased so as not to attract pests.

Many of the fossil plants found in the park are from groups with extant relatives that no longer occur in the United States, consequently a need to develop a leaf comparative collection as part of the paleobotany research program has been identified. This collection may be developed in two possible ways. Traditionally, this would include modern taxa mounted on herbarium sheets and maintained as a modern herbarium collection. This collection would be stored separately from plants originating from within the park. The acquisition of these specimens will be ongoing and it is difficult to estimate the total number of specimens that might be acquired.

Alternatively, new technology would permit the casting of leaves of modern taxa. Depending on the approach followed by the park, this will determine the type of cases for storage and will also impact the IPM plan for the collections, as herbarium specimens would be attractive to pests. Since casts of leaves for reference is a new approach, it is not possible at this time to say how the material would be stored and the consequent demands on available space. As with the modern osteology collection, the park should develop a list of taxa that it would like to acquire for comparative purposes in order to provide an estimate of the number of specimens it might acquire and their related collection needs. This list would be added to the SOCS as an appendix.

Modern Natural History Collections

JODA's modern natural history collections include mammal skins and skeletons in addition to the comparative osteology collection, herbarium collection, and insects preserved in alcohol and dried and pinned. Most of the mammal specimens are housed at the Burke Museum but some are stored at the park; some of the insect collections are stored at Oregon State University. The biology portion of the park collections is minimal and except for minor collections made through the Inventory and Monitoring Program, major growth is not anticipated (Table 6). One area of possible growth would be a set of herbarium sheets of exotic weeds from the park to serve as reference specimens to aid in identification and to document first appearance in the park. Except for the comparative osteology collection, all of the biology collections are currently stored on the third floor of the Cant Ranch House.

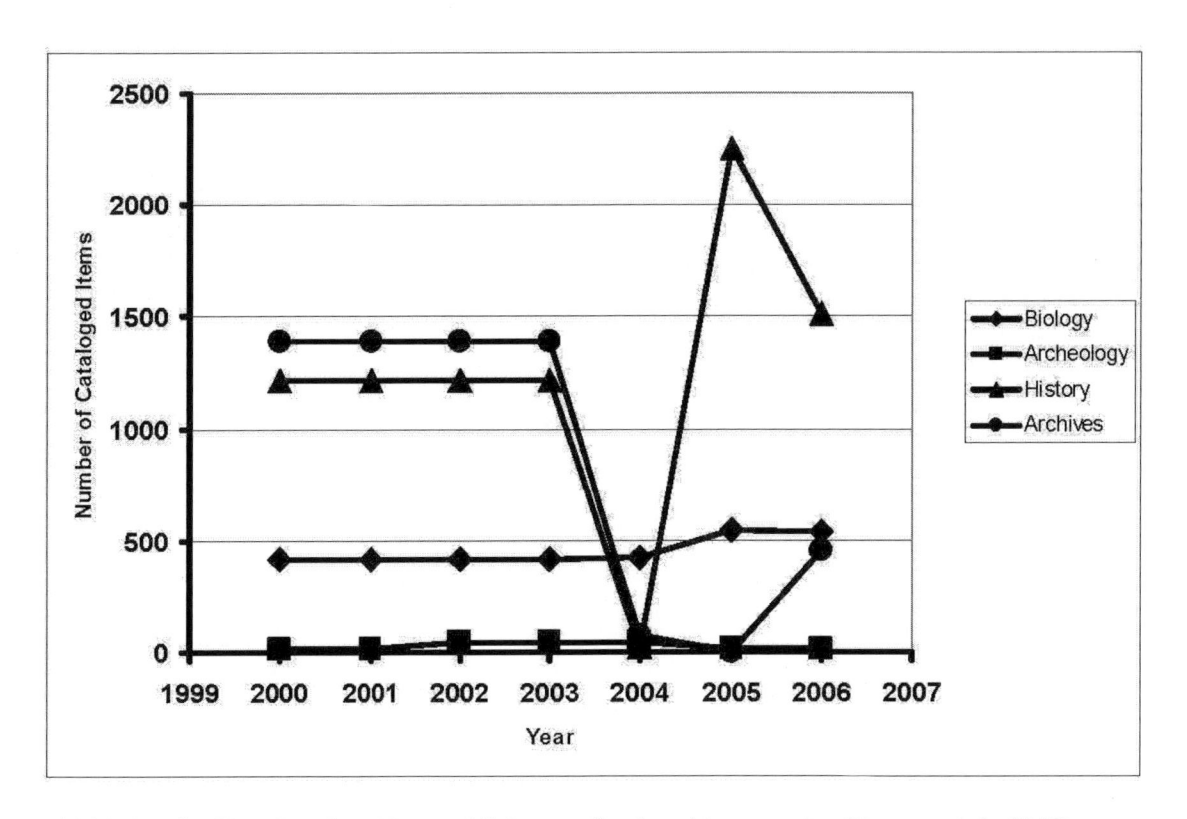

Table 6 Number of cataloged items of biology, archeology, history, and archive records in JODA collections from 2000 to 2006 based on park-submitted CMR

Cultural Collections

It is not anticipated that there will be significant growth of the cultural collections. The collection does not contain any ethnographic material and it is unlikely that any such items appropriate to the park will become available. The historical items on loan from the Cant family and on display will remain property of the family and will not be donated to the park. It is anticipated that ongoing archeological surveys will only produce a moderate increase in the park's collections. Ultimately, most collection growth in this area will be related to archives.

Archeology Collections

Growth of the archeology collections in the park has been minimal (Table 6) in the past. JODA archeological collections provide physical evidence of the long-term cultural heritage of the park, and the central John Day River drainage basin. Collections from site testing and inventory projects contain a variety of chipped stone tools and debitage, plus geological, macrobotanical, and radiocarbon samples related to approximately 10,000 years of human occupation of the region.

A recent survey of all three units of the park has generated a collection of material that will be coming to the park. There are additional materials housed at the University of Oregon that were recovered during Oregon Museum of Science and Industry (OMSI) field school projects in the 1980s and analyzed for Pam Endzweig's dissertation. In addition to these, a number of grinding stones, and perhaps other materials, recovered from these projects in Clarno's Indian Canyon remain stored under the eaves of the paleontology lab at Camp Hancock.

Ongoing surveys provide the potential for more active growth of this part of the collection than has occurred in the past. Presently, these collections are not vast and an appropriate storage location needs to be found within the park. Should a survey result in the discovery of a site that requires active archeological excavations, the resulting volume of material could quickly overwhelm current available collections space at the park. If the collections do grow to any great extent, then another repository will need to be found—perhaps within the Upper Columbia Basin Network (UCBN).

Historical Items

There is no anticipation of a significant increase in the number of historical items added to the park collections. Historical items in the furnished room of the Cant Ranch House are property of the Cant family and there is no indication that they will be donated to the park. The park also has a large number of agricultural implements on-site, many of which are not cataloged. The park should examine and review all of these historic items, both cataloged and uncataloged, for their appropriateness of inclusion in the park collections. It is desirable to have historic items related to ranching within the park boundaries, but if the items do not have a direct relationship to the history of the Cant Ranch, they should not be included in the park collections. If an item is considered to be appropriate for inclusion in the park collections and is cataloged, it should be housed with appropriate environmental conditions. If it is not included in the park collections then its appropriateness as a prop for illustrating some aspect of ranching should be evaluated.

Objects related to park history may also be added to park collections as deemed appropriate but should be reviewed by the park collections committee prior to accessioning.

Historical objects may be obtained for the purposes of exhibits and interpretive programs, but the National Park Service requires that all objects/specimens on exhibit be cataloged into the park collections. To ensure minimal dilution of the park's historic fabric and the introduction of objects unrelated to the park's history, all items obtained for the purposes of exhibit and interpretation should be documented as such and all paperwork related to their origin and acquisition kept on file. When the exhibit is removed, these items can more easily be disposed of because they have no direct provenance to or continuing purpose in the park.

Archives

Based on the current ANCS+ records, archives are underrepresented; they are addressed in Issue B of this report. The updating of the park's archives will have the greatest immediate impact on the park collections in terms of staffing needs, materials and supplies, and space. In addition to the archiving of items related to park research projects, resource management, and administration, the park should also actively include items related to the history of the park such as posters, flyers, and other ephemera. Given the active research program of the park as a condition of any research permits issued to outside researchers, the park should include as deliverables copies of field notes, photographs, maps, stratigraphic cross sections and any other data for inclusion in the park archives. All spatial data from any study should be included as a GIS data layer as appropriate but linked by a finding aid to hard copies in the park archives.

Special Concerns

Orphan Collections

There are many collections of fossils, both public and private, from John Day. Many of these have the potential to become orphan collections; the park is positioned to serve as a repository for these. While it is appropriate for the park to expand its collections from these sources, care must be given to carefully evaluate the collections prior to acquisition. Priority should be given to specimens with:

- associated locality and stratigraphic data;
- well-preserved examples of specific or rare taxa although lacking good associated data;
- specimens from historic collections or associated with historic figures associated with John Day.

Specimens lacking the above qualifications or any other outstanding measure of significance relative to the park mission should not be included in the park collections. Culling of orphan collections should always be considered. Specimens not meeting the minimum qualifications for inclusion in the park collections should be discarded **prior to accessioning the collection.** These specimens can be transferred to the Interpretation Division for educational and interpretive programs.

Educational Collections

While the Interpretation Division may maintain specimens for educational or interpretive purposes, these do not fall under the auspices of NPS museum management policies. Continued handling of these specimens/objects can result in damage and is considered consumptive use. Items from the park collections should not be used for **casual** educational or interpretive purposes given the potential for damage resulting from mishandling. This should not be construed as indicating that park collections should **NEVER** be used for this purpose but only after careful consideration when a specific specimen is required for a specific purpose, and a suitable specimen is not already designated for education and interpretation.

SOP for Acquisition of Items from Outside the Park

Uncontrolled growth of the collection and the inclusion of inappropriate items should be avoided. All items acquired for the purpose of interpretation and education or for exhibits should be clearly identified as such and all records of purchase or how the item was obtained should be preserved. These items should be clearly marked and identified with the IZZ acronym indicating they are part of interpretation and not the park's museum collections.

The park's active molding and casting program can provide the Interpretation Division with high quality casts of rare and fragile specimens such as skulls. While casts of specimens are included in the park collections, casts made specifically for interpretation should not be considered museum objects. In order to avoid misunderstanding as to whether an acquired object should be included in the park collections, the park should establish an Acquisition Committee with individuals representing the museum collections (represented by the park curator), Interpretation and Administration. The committee can evaluate any items acquired from outside the park to meet park needs and evaluate its potential for inclusion in the park collections based on the Park's SOCS.

Housing of holotypes in collections (Museum Management Issue)

The active paleontology research program of the park will result in the description of some specimens as the holotype of new taxa. The park needs to develop a plan on their storage and address their presence in the Emergency Operation and other plans.

Recommendations

- Update and revise the Scope of Collection Statement.
- Revise and update the Paleontological Research Plan to reflect the research accomplished since it was originally written and the subsequent growth of the collections.
- Identify in the revised Paleontological Research Plan all projects that will possibly generate specimens, including potential for rate of recovery of specimens (recognizing that some formations/sites have a higher density of specimens then others) that may be found, and those

projects that will only produce archival data, both field records and lab reports.

- Evaluate environmental and storage needs of all collections not related to the paleontology program, potential growth and potential costs associated with their care. Based on this data determine if it would be preferable to house these items with a partner repository.

- Working with appropriate experts, including the local ranching community, evaluate the farm machinery currently located at the Cant Ranch.

- Review current holdings of park collections in outside repositories, determine if park should develop Repository Agreement with new partners (such as the University of Oregon for the archeology collections), if only a loan agreement is needed, or if the collections should be moved to another location. Determine which items currently housed at the park could be transferred to partner repositories for storage. This should include an analysis of possible costs associated with curatorial needs of collections at partner repository.

- Establish a park collections committee to review all acquisitions from outside the park. Ensure that all objects obtained from outside the park intended for interpretation, education, or exhibit are clearly marked and all documentation pertaining to their acquisition is preserved so they are not mistakenly added to the museum collections later.

- Accession and catalog all materials acquired for exhibit purposes into the park museum collection.

Figure 8 Library

Appendix A—
Archives, Library, and Museum Collections Survey Results

This appendix details the results of the survey relating to the archives and collections management program at John Day Fossil Beds National Monument. The survey was conducted in advance of the MMP team's visit in an effort to identify and quantify staff needs relating to the park archives, museum collections, and library programs.

Survey Objectives

The primary objectives of the survey were to determine the following:

- Percentage of the staff using the park library and museum collections
- Percentage of the staff using non-park information resources
- Primary areas (categories) of information use, and the reasons for use of those specific collections
- Primary reasons the staff *do not* use these information resources, and what actions may be necessary to promote resource availability and use

In addition, limited demographic information was collected to develop a length of service and experience profile, and to demonstrate equitable response from each park administrative unit.

Survey Methodology

The target universe of the survey was the permanent and temporary staff of JODA. The survey was distributed to 19 park staff members in Spring 2007, requesting that the survey be completed and returned to the Paleontologist prior to June 1. A total of 10 responses were returned, representing a 58% response rate. A response rate of 12% is required for this type of survey to be considered statistically valid, so the JODA response should be considered legitimate, with a high degree of confidence in the results. Responses were not as well distributed across park work units as could be hoped; 50% of the response was from the Paleontology and Resources Management staffs, and 20% from Interpretation. There was no response from the divisions of Administration, Maintenance, or Law Enforcement. Sixty percent of the respondents were permanent staff, whereas 30% were from park volunteer staff.

The primary method used for information gathering was a checklist, with some additional supporting data gathered by filling in blanks with quantitative information.

Respondents were also given limited opportunities to add written comment. Write-in responses are generally not used in surveys of this type, as they often fail to elicit a statistically valid response, and the response that is generated is often difficult to quantify. This proved to be the case with this particular survey, where most of the written responses were anecdotal in nature, and tended to reinforce information already recorded by the respondents in the checklist sections.

Since the response to the survey in general (58%) was sufficient to be considered statistically valid, the results will be considered representative to the survey population as a whole. Percentages have been rounded up to equal numbers when 0.5 or more, and rounded down when less than 0.5.

Demographics

Demographic information can assist with understanding motivation and needs of the respondents, in addition to documenting an adequate distribution of response across administrative division and employment status. Information collected from this survey included length of service, distribution by administrative unit, and employment status.

Length of service

	Total	Average
Years of service	118	11
Years at JODA	80	8
Years in current position	63	6

Distribution by administrative unit

Administration	0
Interpretation	2
Maintenance	0
Law Enforcement	0
Paleontology	3
Resource Management	1
Unknown[1]	4

Employment status

Temporary / Seasonal	0
Permanent	6
Non NPS Employees	3
Unknown[2]	1

Notes from the Tables Above:

[1] Two VIP respondents did not specify which division/s they work with; one respondent (Permanent Staff) checked all administrative units; one other respondent (Permanent Staff) did not complete his/her survey.

[2] One respondent (Permanent Staff) did not complete his/her survey.

Survey Summaries

When reviewing survey results it is important to remember that a response rate of 12% is considered necessary for the results of the survey as a whole to be considered as valid. Within the survey, a 10% response to any given section or question is necessary for the response to be considered significant. Naturally this significance increases with the number of responses to the section or question. For these reasons the results provided below are phrased in terms of percentages of the respondents to any given section or question. The following list shows the percentage of use of the collections by park staff responding (10 responses):

- 90% used the library an average of 33 times last year (22% of these respondents used the library 100 or more times last year).
- 90% used the archives and museum collections an average of 43 times last year.

    Note: This average is highly distorted upward, as one third of the respondents use the collections far in excess of the other six—one uses the collections every day (260 times per annum) while two used the collection fifty times per year. Collections use among the other six respondents averages five times per year.

- 70% used non-service archives, library, or museum collections an average of 59 times last year. This number also is highly distorted due to the following circumstances concerning use and incomplete survey forms:

    1) Two respondents (which comprise 28%) use the collections far in excess of the other five—one used non-service archives, library, or museum collections 300 times last year, while the other used such facilities 100 times.

    2) Two respondents did not state the number of times s/he accessed non-NPS resources.

    3) Use among the other three respondents averaged five times per year.

The majority of the staff uses the library and a significant percentage of the staff uses the archival and museum collections in some aspects of their jobs. In addition 70% of the responding staff is using archival, museum, and library resources located outside the park. It might be interesting to determine what services are *not* being offered by the park that requires this number of the staff to use outside sources for needed reference. This could be accomplished by a one-sheet survey to all employees requesting specific information for improving services (title/subject suggestions for books/periodicals, hours of operation, etc.).

A total of 9 respondents (90% of the total response universe) indicated they used the archives and museum collections. The top five types of collections indicated as being used by this group are as follows:

- 80% - Paleontological fossils and traces
- 70% - Photographs and images

- 60% - Geological rocks, minerals, samples
- 60% - Natural records, maps, images, reports
- 40% - Herbarium/plants (a tie)
- 40% - Park cultural resource records (a tie)

The same respondents as above indicated the following as the primary reasons for using the collections:

- 80% - Personal learning
- 60% - Address internal NPS information needs
- 60% - Identification and comparison
- 50% - Develop interpretive programs
- 50% - Develop exhibit

These results document that the primary resources used are the paleontological collections, and that the primary reasons for use are an interesting mixture that includes both personal and vocational motivations.

Section II of the survey considered reasons staff may not use the resources and suggestions for improvement in the way these resources are managed and made available for use. The full universe of the 10 park staff responding was considered, and respondents were allowed as many statements as they felt applied. The results were as follows:

- 80% - Improve electronic access to museum collection data and object information.
- 70% - Provide on-line or remote access to databases.
- 60% - Staff the collection with at least one professional position.
- 60% - Provide additional professional staff to organize and work on collections.
- 40% - Provide listings and finding aids of what is in the museum collection.
- 30% - Provide remote computer access to collections/archives.
- 30% - Improve the preservation and physical condition of the collections.

Through the responses in this section the park staff have identified what they consider to be the major detractors to the current museum management operation, and identified actions they would see as positive improvements.

In addition, the staff supports expending staff time and funding for the management of park archives, collections, and libraries (an aggregate of 60% indicating that additional staffing was required for management and access).

General Conclusions

The park libraries and museum collections receive a much higher than normal incidence of use when compared to that of other parks. Park staff indicated a need for the resources and information that well-defined and administered collections can provide.

As a result, the park should be looking at ways to facilitate access through the use of innovative strategies to provide for additional museum staff to assist collections users; production of finding aids (including some type of online presence); the joint housing of archives, collections, and library resources; and providing several methods of intellectual access to the park specific resources.

A general informational finding aid should be produced for distribution to the park staff at the earliest opportunity. Some of the specialized features of the ANCS+ program should help with this. This should be followed by subject matter specific finding aids as they are able to be produced.

The survey format provided the park staff with the opportunity to offer individual impressions of the archives, museum collections, and library program operations in a candid manner, as well as providing a venue for staff suggestions for changes and improvement. The survey results provide park management with firm background data that should be useful in developing specific programs to manage these unique park resources.

Appendix B—
Suggested Workload Analysis

This appendix provides an example of a system for analyzing the museum management program work elements for JODA. By completing this chart the total staffing needs will be documented. Additional work elements relating to park records management, library, and the permit process could be added.

Core Work Elements	Current (Hours)	Current (FTE)	Needed (Hours)	Needed (FTE)	Non-Pers. $
Acquisition of Collections					
Plan strategy for acquisition					
Identify sources of collections					
Survey for inclusion in Park collections					
Appraisal and evaluation of proposed acquisitions					
Manage acquisition committee					
Manage Park records					
Acquire rights and permission					
Subtotal					
Documentation of collections					
Accession new acquisitions within two (2) weeks					
Process archival collections including completion of ANCS+ catalog records					
Catalog museum objects					
Catalog library materials					

John Day Fossil Beds National Monument

Photograph museum collections					
Maintain museum documentation					
Manage databases/knowledge systems					
Maintain documentation of treatment, use, etc.					
Maintain NAGPRA information					
Subtotal					
Preservation and protection of collections					
Maintain facility					
Provide for physical and operation security					
Ensure fire protection					
Monitor environment					
Monitor pests					
Ensure disaster preparedness					
Conduct housekeeping					
Ensure proper storage, including organization, equipment, and housing					
Conduct conservation program by assessing collection condition					
Treat items in need					
Subtotal					
Access and use of collections					
Provide for public and Park access including reference services					

Develop and maintain exhibits					
Participate in curriculum-based education programs					
Conduct public program					
Produce publications					
Conduct research and obtain legal rights and permissions					
Loan collections for appropriate use by other institutions					
Develop and maintain internet/intranet access and website(s)					
Participate in NPS planning and compliance					
Conduct research					
Support appropriate reproduction of collections					
Subtotal					
Program administration and management					
Maintain up-to-date scope of collection statement					
Complete annual reporting: Collection Management Report; Annual Inventory; ANCS+ Database					
Manage annual budget					
Provide for future programming: PMIS and OFS					
Supervise paid and unpaid staff					
Develop and maintain up-to-date museum plans and policies					
Manage contracts					

Maintain information technology/management					
Provide administrative support					
Participate in Park management and administrative issues					
Subtotal					
Total					

Appendix C — Possible Non-NPS Funding Sources

The following is a sampling of organizations which might provide funding for museum and paleontological programs at JODA. Note that some of the federal granting agencies will not grant directly to a federal agency, but by working with a partner, projects might be funded through them. They may also be the source of VIPs or interns. The American Association of Museums (aam.org) also has a list of granting organizations with direct links to their websites.

Botanical Society of America (BSA) – The BSA is a membership society whose mission is to promote botany, the field of basic science dealing with the study and inquiry into the form, function, development, diversity, reproduction, evolution, and uses of plants and their interactions within the biosphere. There are 15 special interest sections of the Society, including paleobotany. P.O. Box 299, St. Louis, MO 63166   botany.org/

Department of Education (ED) – This federal agency provides grants for a number of education programs. ED's mission is to promote student achievement and preparation for global competitiveness by fostering educational excellence and ensuring equal access. 400 Maryland Avenue SW, Washington, DC 20202   ed.gov/index.html

Earthwatch Institute – Earthwatch Institute is an international non-profit organization that brings science to life for people concerned about the Earth's future. Earthwatch supports scientific field research by offering volunteers the opportunity to join research teams around the world. 3 Clock Tower Place, Maynard, MA 01754-0075   earthwatch.org/

Evolving Earth Foundation – This foundation is dedicated to promoting earth science-related education and research. PO BOX 2090, Issaquah, WA 98027   evolvingearth.org/

Geological Society of America (GSA) – The mission of GSA is to be a leader in advancing the geosciences, enhancing the professional growth of its members, and promoting the geosciences in the service of humankind. GSA also sponsors the GeoCorps America program, which subsidizes, recruits, and administers paleontology internships in national parks. PO Box 9140, Boulder, CO 80301-9140   geosociety.org/

Institute of Museum and Library Services (IMLS) – The Institute's mission is to create strong libraries and museums that connect people to information and ideas. The Institute works at the national level and in coordination with state and local organizations to sustain heritage, culture, and knowledge; enhance learning and innovation; and support professional development. As a federal agency, they do not provide direct funding to federal agencies. 1800 M Street NW, 9th Floor, Washington, DC 20036 imls.gov/index.htm

National Endowment for the Humanities (NEH) – NEH is an independent grant-making agency of the United States government dedicated to supporting research, education, preservation, and public programs in the humanities. As a federal agency, they do not provide direct funding to federal agencies. 1100 Pennsylvania Ave., NW, Washington, DC 20506   neh.gov/index.html

National Geographic Society – The Society's Mission Programs support critical expeditions and scientific fieldwork; encourage geography education for students; promote natural and cultural conservation; and inspire audiences through new media, vibrant exhibitions, and live events. P.O. Box 98199, Washington, D.C. 20090-8199   nationalgeographic.com/index.html)

National Park Foundation (NPF) – The mission of the Foundation is to strengthen the enduring connection between the American people and their National Parks by raising private funds, making strategic grants, creating innovative partnerships, and increasing public awareness. 1201 Eye Street, NW, Suite 550B, Washington, DC 20005 nationalparks.org/Home.asp

National Science Foundation (NSF) – The National Science Foundation (NSF) is an independent federal agency created by Congress in 1950 "to promote the progress of science; to advance the national health, prosperity, and welfare; to secure the national defense…" As a federal agency, they do not provide direct funding to federal agencies.
4201 Wilson Boulevard, Arlington, Virginia 22230   nsf.gov/

Northwest Interpretive Association (NWIA) – NWIA is a nonprofit organization dedicated to increasing public appreciation of the rich cultural history and spectacular natural beauty of the Pacific Northwest. NWIA helps the National Park Service, the US Forest Service, and other public land agencies provide high quality educational materials to the visiting public.   164 S. Jackson St., Seattle, WA 98104
nwpubliclands.org/

Oregon Public Lands Institute (OPLI) – Protects, promotes, and educates about Oregon's ancient and living landscapes including the Earth's most accessible place to view the past 40 million years of life, while supporting the rural communities of the John Day Basin.
401 W. 4th Street, P.O. Box 104, Fossil, OR 97830
oregonpaleoproject.org/

Save America's Treasures (SAT) – The National Park Service granting program for the protection of our nation's endangered and irreplaceable and endangered cultural heritage.   Heritage Preservation Services, National Park Service, 1201 "Eye" Street, NW, 6th Floor [ORG. 2256], Washington, D.C. 20005   cr.nps.gov/hps/treasures/

The Paleontological Society – The Paleontological Society is an international organization devoted exclusively to the advancement of the science of paleontology.   Department of Earth and Environment, Franklin & Marshall College, Lancaster, Pennsylvania 17604   paleosoc.org/

The Society of Vertebrate Paleontology (SVP) – SVP is organized exclusively for educational and scientific purposes, with the object of advancing the science of vertebrate paleontology.   60 Revere Dr. Suite 500, Northbrook, IL 60062   vertpaleo.org/

Appendix D — Preliminary Survey of Park Archives

BUILDING	ROOM	CABINET	MATERIALS	QUANTITY
Cant Ranch House	3rd Floor	On open shelving	Oversize site, planning and parcel maps, building and utility plans, drawings, as-builts	Approximately 200 items (multi-page sets counted as 1 item)
		On open shelving	Central Files, budget and other permanent records in boxes	5 linear feet (LF)
		Cab 1	Historic Resource Study materials, misc. documents stored flat on bottom shelf	2 LF
		Cab 2	Sleeved photo negatives	1067 items
		4-drawer metal card cabinet	Corresponding photo prints mounted on cards	1067 items
		Cab 2	Oral history Tapes 1982-1984	26 cassettes
	Historians Office	Closet & desk drawer	Oral History Tapes 1970s-1980s, transcripts, exhibit planning records, misc	60 cassettes + 1.5 LF
	Administrative Offices	2 brown lateral file cabinets	Central Files: appraise re NPS #19, identify active records sets, select inactive records for inclusion in archives, schedule appropriate records for destruction	23 LF
	Resource Managers Office	In office file drawers and shelves, map holder and auxiliary closet	Resource management maps, topographic maps, park reports generated by resource management staff and contractors, xxx forms	6 LF of slides in binders + 15-20 rolled maps + 3 LF of park reports & files
	Superintendents Office		Maps, plans, drawings	50 oversize items

BUILDING	ROOM	CABINET	MATERIALS	QUANTITY
TCPC	Collections Storage Room in Paleo	Flat files Drawers 1-3, 5-10 (Drawer 4 –aerials & overlays- is cataloged)	Transects and overlays; master locality sheets; color aerials; topographical, boundary, parcel, geology, land status, and tract maps; TCPC site planning drawings; animal drawings	Approx 100-150 items (multi-page sets counted as 1 item)
		2 slide storage cabinets	Slides	Approx 2000 slides
		Gray File Cabinet Dr 2	Project and other files and materials needing appraisal	1 LF
		Visual Storage Cabinet 7	Binders with original images published as book plates, GIS spatial data notebooks	2 LF
	Accessions Room in Paleo	Brown 2-door Cabinet on wall	Slides, videos, park reports, reprints	6 LF
		Brown 2-door Cabinet on wall	Theses, dissertations, aerials	3 LF
	Chief of Interp Office	Two 5-drawer vertical file cabinets	Files include program management, publications and projects, exhibits info and reference materials brought by Chief from other duty stations.	15 LF
	Interp Main office	Shelves	Videos, both produced and homemade; 8 mm films; binders with b/w prints, slides	6 LF of videos & film and photos
Barn	Interp cache	On floor and shelves	4 large cartons of materials including films, manuals, trail statistics, visitor survey data, misc files	12 LF
LE Rangers Office		Files	Past written annual reports, plans and misc files	Undetermined (probably less than 1 LF)

BUILDING	ROOM	CABINET	MATERIALS	QUANTITY
Library	In restricted area	Shelves & boxes	Rare books	10-20 items
	Main area	Shelves near periodicals	Plans and reports generated by or about the park, shelf files with misc admin history docs and other donations	2 LF
	First row	Shelf files	Cant Ranch Oral history monographs	3 LF
TOTALS			TOTALS	4,410 items + 90 linear feet + 350 oversize documents

These materials were identified by NPS Archivist Carola DeRooy during a preliminary survey of park offices in June of 2007. The materials listed are those requiring appraisal using *NPS DO #19, Records Disposition Schedule*. A qualified archivist can review this material to further identify active records sets, select materials that are inactive or require higher levels of protection for inclusion in archives, and schedule appropriate records for destruction that have met their retention period. Some materials should be transferred to the library. The list does not include digital record sets, image sets and databases in all divisions, which should also undergo appraisal.

Appendix E — NPS Records Management

The underpinning philosophy and paradigm of records management within the National Park Service is being rethought in light of NPS best practices and continuing technological impacts on communications. The Department of the Interior (DOI) and NPS have identified the need for continuing management of Park cultural and natural resources in two concepts: "Mission Critical Records," as presented in *Director's Order 19 (DO#19)* and "Resource Management Records," as presented in the DOI and National Park Service museum management policies.

DO#19 specifically identifies mission critical records as having the highest priority in records management activities. Mission critical records are all records documenting natural and cultural resources and their previous management. These records contain information crucial for the future management of the resources and include "general management plans and other major planning documents that record basic management and philosophies and policies, or that direct Park management and activities for long periods of time." Other examples of mission critical records include records that directly support the specific mission of a Park unit and the overall mission of the National Park Service. These records are permanent records that will eventually become archival records. Therefore, *DO#19* dictates that these records should receive archival care as soon as practical in their life cycle.

Similar to that of mission critical records is the concept of "resource management records." The DOI manual's definition says that resource management records are "made or acquired by the federal government to record information on cultural and natural resources." As described in the *Cultural Resource Management Guideline (NPS-28)*, resource management records document Park resources and serve as key information for their continuing management. Accordingly, they are classified as "library and museum materials made or acquired and preserved solely for reference or exhibition purposes." Therefore, these materials are excluded from the National Archives' definition of records.

However, in the last few years, the definition of resource management records has broadened beyond reference or exhibition materials. Many official records have also been designated as important for the long-term management of park cultural and natural resources. In the past, official records could not be added to a park's museum or library collection. But records generated by the planning process and compliance review actions of resource management are important official records that never reach an inactive status.

The past system of records management and disposition as promulgated in *NPS-19* focused on "official records" and "unofficial records." Official records were original documents created or received by a park in the course of performing the daily business of the NPS. Unofficial records encompassed duplicate copies of official records and documents generated in association with a resource management project (e.g., archeological field notes). Non-official records were materials not created by a government agency, and included donated manuscripts (e.g., letters written by an eminent figure associated with the creation of a park), collections of personal papers, organizational records of non-governmental entities such as businesses or civic groups, and collections accrued by private individuals.

Only unofficial and non-official records could be placed in a park's museum collection, after evaluation against the park's Scope of Collection Statement (SOCS) for retention, if appropriate. By law National Archives and Records Administration (NARA) has been responsible for the official records of the federal government, once the records are no longer actively needed and have reached their disposition date. Non-official records, such as manuscript collections, were not governed by the NPS Records Disposition Schedule and NARA and included in a park's museum collection based upon its SOCS.

Under the new methodology, instead of a record's importance being primarily dictated by its form (a signed original or a copy), a record's primary importance is to be determined by the actual information it carries. This philosophy divides records into "permanent" and "temporary;" copies are to be considered just copies and so are not addressed. Permanent records have continuing value to resource management. Temporary records have a limited use life in the operations of a Park (or support office).

There is also discussion of the notion of "permanently active" records, those materials needed for the long-term, ongoing management of park resources for the NPS to fulfill its agency mandate. The criteria for permanent and temporary also take into account the office of creation—a permanent record for one office, such as a regional office, may be temporary for a park because it is a distributed copy for general reference only. Temporary records are to be retained as long as indicated by the revised Records Retention Schedule. After their allotted retention time, temporary records may be disposed of by parks or retained longer if still needed.

Many of the disposition time frames outlined in *NPS-19* have been retained in the new *DO#19* retention schedule. This applies in particular to fiscal, routine administrative, law enforcement, forms covered under NARA General Records Schedule 20, and other daily operational materials. Permanent records may also be retained as long as actively needed for use and reference. Under the new *DO#19*, permanent records are to include land acquisition records, park planning documents, documents pertaining to cultural and resource management decisions and projects, and documents pertaining to the history of the administration and interpretation of a park.

The concept of resource management records has been broadened in *DO#19* from definitions in *NPS-19* that classified only associated project records as permanent, such as archeological field notes and natural history project data. Currently, the National Park Service Records Advisory Council (RAC) has suspended disposition of certain official records that may be important for parks to retain on-site. The new, broadened concept classifies as permanent a wide array of documents previously considered temporary (such as construction reports) because the subject of the document is a park resource or substantially impacts a park resource. Thus, for example, previously all contracts were considered temporary, whereas the broadened definition of resource management records considers contracts on cultural resources (e.g., a historic building on the National Register of Historic Places) permanent.

Under the new NARA protocol, parks will have three avenues to choose among to provide accessibility to their inactive (no longer actively needed or in use) records before the records are permanently destroyed or retired to the National Archives. Under the new proposal, parks may still send inactive records to a NARA Federal Records Center for public access and storage following the current procedure, but now a fee will be charged by the Office of Management and Budget ($3.28 per cubic foot as of Oct. 2000). This charge is currently being paid by WASO for all parks.

Parks can now arrange for storage at an off-site commercial repository, or to retain their own records on-site. In both cases, professional archival parameters of preservation and access set by NARA must be met. These archival parameters include security, fire protection, appropriate storage techniques, climate controlled environment, and widely disseminated collection finding aids. Once the inactive records have reached their disposition date, records are to be destroyed or transferred to the National Archives for permanent storage. These new changes in records definitions and storage procedures will not be reflected in *DO#28 Cultural Resources Management Guideline* and the *NPS Museum Handbook,* Part II, Appendix D, "Museum Archives and Manuscript Collections," until these documents are revised.

Records managers recommend parks establish comprehensive, stand-alone project files for resource management, major special events, park infrastructure and research projects, and that these project files not be assigned NPS file codes. These files should contain copies of finalized contract documents including substantive change orders and specifications, DI-1's, "as-builts" for finished construction projects, related project planning documents, and all documents illustrating all decisions made and why.

For research projects, project files should also include copies of all researcher field notes, laboratory notes and results, a copy of the final report and report drafts, and any other materials generated by the project in question. Thus, staff are assured that a full set of documents covering an entire project are gathered, in order of creation and project evolution, in one place. It also averts problems when some fiscal records are filed separately from other project materials, thus potentially loosing critical data from a project's life history. These project files, upon completion of the project, should then be retired to the park's museum archives for long-term reference. The separation of routine administrative records from project records is recommended practice in the General Records Schedules as well. NARA expects that routine administrative records are temporary with short retention spans before destruction. Project records, on the other hand, are expected to have long retention periods, be permanent, and have potential (if not anticipated) archival value.

The *Museum Handbook,* Part II, Appendix D, "Museum Archives and Manuscript Collections," governing the creation and management of park archives and manuscript collections, does not reflect this paradigm shift. It reflects the guidelines of *NPS-19*, and states that non-official records, or only "associated project records," are eligible to be retained by a park for its museum collection archives. The new paradigm is also not reflected in *DO#28, Cultural Resources Management Guideline.* Both Appendix D and *DO#28* will be revised to reflect the changes in NARA policy and NPS records management upon their finalization.

Appendix F—
Preparing Inactive Records for Transfer to Storage

The records management program is able to assist park divisions, branches, and offices to professionally and legally manage the records created and received in the course of performing the park's business. This program can provide legal and technical advice regarding the management of records in offices as well as in park retention storage locations housing inactive records. Retention periods for National Park Service records are specified either in the General Records Schedule (GRS), the Federal Government's guideline on retention/disposition of records common to all government agencies, and *NPS-19, Records Management Guideline,* Appendix B, Records Retention Schedule.

It is the responsibility of each park office wishing to retire inactive records to fully prepare them to the specifications that follow before they may be transferred to the park museum collection. Once this is done, the park curator or his/her representative will visit the office to verify the preparation and physically transfer the records to the museum collection. Of course, park museum staff will be happy to provide assistance in the interpretation of these instructions at any time during the preparation of records for transfer.

- No records are to be dropped off at the curator's office without full prior preparation and approval of the curator.
- Records received unannounced or unprepared will be returned to the owning office.

ALL files pertaining to agency business are government property, not the property of the individual employee.

Preparing Records for Transfer

- Use only approved GSA Records Storage Boxes, NSN 8115-00-117-8249, or approved archival boxes. These boxes can be ordered through GSA for large quantities of records, or the park museum may be able to provide boxes if only a few are required.

- Remove all files from hanging folders and three-ring binders. Place in appropriately sized (legal or letter) folders that fully contain the records without folding. Any file exceeding one inch in thickness, such as thick files contained in binders, must be split between multiple folders (place in two or more folders). This rule does not apply to Contracting Project files, which are self-contained packages and may be thicker. Number multiple folders "F1/2, F2/2", etc.

- Make certain EVERY folder has a clear label, typed or neatly handwritten, indicating a clear, descriptive title of the contents, the date or date range of the file and, preferably, a file code and retention period. NPS file codes are not mandatory, but they make records review and disposition actions must faster and simpler and provide a common scheme for filing of related documents. File codes are not necessarily appropriate for project files as they may contain a large variety of materials that do not fit within a file code.

- Remove all personal materials and multiple copies of documents (keep no more than two). Remove all blank forms.

- Remove all office supplies and computer materials such as desk supplies, computer manuals, miscellaneous diskettes, etc.

- Consult with Records Management staff for assistance with odd-size and unusual format materials such as engineering drawings, photographs, audio and videotapes, etc. Do not combine these materials in boxes with standard-sized records in folders, unless they are an integral part of a particular file. NEVER fold oversize materials to fit into record storage boxes.

Electronic Records

Many word-processed and other types of documents are now received in electronic format and are used that way in park offices. The preservation of records in electronic format is a very problematic issue, one which much larger agencies are having difficulty grappling with. The park curator advises all park departments that preserving records in electronic format is not possible at this time, as neither the hardware nor software capability to do so is available.

Make sure to print hard copy of critical and important records and interfile them with the related paper records. Hard copy records have a proven history of preservation capability. The curator will be happy to discuss the management of databases in electronic form for long-term storage and preservation. All electronic mail and word processing documents that must be retained for either temporary legal purposes or are permanently valuable as archival materials MUST be printed and transferred to records storage in hard copy format.

Records Series and Records Disposition

In archives and records management terminology, records are dealt with in groupings called "series." A series is a group of records which may be defined either by format or conditions of creation or use. A more formal definition may be "file units or documents arranged according to a filing system or kept together because they relate to a particular subject or function, result from the same activity, document a specific kind of transaction, take a particular physical form, or have some other relationship arising out of their creation, receipt, or use, such as restrictions on access and use." A records series is generally handled as a unit for disposition purposes.[3]

Examples of series in National Park Service records include: contract project files; time and attendance records; alphabetical subject files; purchase orders; and press releases. Records are handled in series because these categories may be designated within the National Park Service Records Disposition Schedule for authorized legal periods of retention. Some series (such as budget, human resources, and contracting) records may be destroyed after keeping for a certain period for legal purposes. Other types of records, generally all records dealing with management of resources and administrative decision process, etc., have permanent value and are retained as archives collections. For this reason, the museum staff asks that records be managed and retired in identifiable series to increase the ease of handling when assigning retention periods and, later, in destroying or transferring records to appropriate locations.

---

[3] Definitions provided in this paragraph are taken from Appendix D: Glossary, Disposition of Federal Records: A Records Management Handbook, Washington, DC: National Archives and Records Administration, 1992.

"Disposition" in records management is defined as "the actions taken regarding records no longer needed for current government business." These actions can include transfer to storage facilities, destruction, or transfer to archives. In this instance, "disposition" does not automatically mean destruction.

Packing Records for Transfer

Try to place only one record series with one disposition date in a box. Records will later be disposed of by box, not by removing individual files from boxes. *Example:* Place all retiring DI-1s in a group of boxes. This is one 'series' of records, all one document type with all the same destruction date. If a single series doesn't fill a box, different series may be combined in a box for space economy, as long as they are clearly labeled.

Pack the files in the same sequence in the cartons as they are arranged in the file drawer, using the same filing system as that used in the office. Place folders with labels facing the front of the box (label area), or facing to the right of front if the folders are legal sized.

Do not over pack boxes. One must be able to slip a hand easily between folders and get into the hand-holds. If this is not possible, the box is too full.

Label each box as it is filled. Label only in PENCIL! Labeling should consist of the following: the owning office symbol plus fiscal year in the upper left hand corner label area and the sequential number in the upper right hand corner. Number sequentially, e.g., 1/12, 2/12, etc. If it is unknown how many boxes there will be, just enter the sequence number, then add the whole number to all boxes after completion of the packing job, e.g., 1/, 2/, 3/, 4/, then go back and add in the total box count at the end: 1/4, 2/4, 3/4, 4/4. The office may contact the museum staff for assigning a unique accession number prior to ascertaining boxes are fully identifiable, especially if multiple groupings of records, or series, will be retired at the same time. Each series group will be assigned a unique number by the museum staff for control purposes and to facilitate later destruction or other action. A fully labeled box may resemble this example:

ACP-99-2   BPA Records   Box ½

This example identifies the second group of records (the "2" is assigned by the Records Center) retired from the Contracting & Procurement Office in Fiscal Year 99, which consists of BPA Records and is the first of two boxes in this grouping to be prepared and retired to the Records Center.

For security, as well as neatness, do not identify the contents of the box on the outside, beyond the simple title shown in the example above. The detailed contents will be outlined in the inventory document.

When packing records, do not stack boxes over four high, any higher tends to begin crushing the boxes. A stack of four boxes can easily be loaded on a hand truck for transport without additional handling.

Preparing Records Inventory or Transfer List

Prepare a records transfer document consisting of a general list of the contents and boxes. A detailed listing of folders is not needed because this information will be entered into the master database at the park museum. If everything is well labeled, this database input can occur very quickly at the museum, and a printed copy of the inventory will be returned to the office for incorporation into the Department's Inactive Records Binder. This is a good chance to double-check to ensure that adequate and consistent labeling has been applied to ALL folders in the box. The general listing may provide the name of the records series, the date range of the records, the number of boxes in the group to be retired, and disposition information if known, also any information that may assist the museum staff in preparing or managing the files during their retirement period.

Where there are multiple folders of a single records title and date range, they will be listed in the database inventory as a group as shown below rather than individually for space and time efficiency. Please ensure that related groupings are appropriately marked with sequential folder numbers, e.g. 1/3, 2/3, 3/3. The inventory listing will appear as:

BPA File - Ace Hardware - 3 folders

Some types of documents have their own unique number sequences, such as contract files, purchase order files, and time and attendance files by pay period. These types of documents may continue to be in folders as they were in the department (e.g., accordion folders containing all time sheets for a single pay period, etc.). The complete number range of such documents should be correctly listed on the folders, so when the folder headings are used to create the inventory, the information is complete and correct. When preparing the inventory, list the documents in their normal numbering sequence. Consult with records management staff for assistance.

Transferring Prepared Records to the Park Museum

After all above steps have been completed, contact the curator to request physical transfer of the records. The curator or a member of the records staff will come to review the preparations and physically transfer the records to the park museum.

The records always should be physically transferred by museum staff, to protect against damage or loss to the records or personal injury during moving.

An appointment will be scheduled to complete the physical transfer to the park museum. Depending on the current demand, pick-ups may be delayed because of other records intake actions in progress which may be occupying the limited workspace. Records will be picked up as quickly as possible. PLEASE do not move the records to a dangerous storage environment while waiting for pick-up! This includes any basement or unheated building in the Park.

After-Transfer Actions

Museum staff will review records boxes and transfer documentation, and make any necessary corrections. Museum staff will perform database entry of the individual file folders in the records accession. Finalized copies of the inventories and transfer forms will be placed on file in the park museum with a tickler system for later action on the records. The staff will send a printout of the completed inventory back to the office, along with a revised Table of Contents for the Department Inactive Records Binder including the newly accessioned and processed material. Please follow the instructions with the inventory and in the Records Binder to incorporate this new material into your department's binder.

Records that are retired by park offices to the park museum remain the property of the office. They will not be available for research to anyone except that office's personnel without the express written permission of the office head.

Records that need to be recalled by the office should be referred to by the accession number, the box number, and the folder title as listed on the records inventory in your department's Inactive Records Binder.

Office staff may request the return of records for a period of 30 days, renewable, or a photocopy of the records. This is to ensure that retrieved records do not become lost and unavailable for further review as needed. One office employee must sign for the records to ensure accountability during the time they are removed from storage.

As scheduled review dates for the records come up, the museum staff will communicate with the owning office regarding the ongoing value of the records for government business. Reviews should occur approximately every two years. These reviews form the basis for further records actions which are normal in the life cycle of records. Many financial and human resources records may be destroyed within a certain period of years. The Records Action Form will initiate further actions, such as a decision to retain records in the park museum for additional time, for destruction, or for transfer of permanently valuable records to the park's archives.

Appendix G — Archiving Transfer of Resource Management Field Records to Museum Archives

Suggested Standard Operating Procedure

The purpose of this SOP is to aid park staff in accomplishing their responsibilities according to *DO#77 (Natural Resources Management Guideline), DO#28 (Cultural Resources Management Guideline), DM 411 (DOI Property Management Regulations), DO#19 (Records Management Guideline)*, 36 CFR 2.9, and legislation associated with archiving resource management records.

The [name of park's] Museum Management Plan documents the need for guidelines on the management of archival material. Recommendations include retention of reports of archeological, historical, architectural, and other scientific research conducted within and for the park.

The parks' archives include many unique information resources that need professional organization and arrangement to promote their most efficient use. Park resource management staffs generate records on a daily basis that should be considered for inclusion in the park archives. Staff is creating data sets, photographs, maps, and field notebooks that future generations will need to access to research the history of cultural and natural resource projects at the parks.

Park staff are involved in capturing fire monitoring data, plant collections, air quality research, and a host of ethnographic and archeological research. Preserving the corporate knowledge of each of these individual activities depends ultimately upon the archival process. The organizing thread, then, should be the project itself.

Archeological Records

Government-wide regulations for the curation and care of federal archeological collections required by the National Historic Preservation Act (NHPA), the Reservoir Salvage Act, and the Archeological Resources Protection Act (ARPA) were issued in 1990 as "Curation of Federally Owned and Administered Archeological Collections" (36 CFR 79). These regulations establish procedures and guidelines to manage and preserve collections. They also include terms and conditions for federal agencies to include in contracts and cooperative agreements with non-federal repositories. This document covers excavations done under the authority or in connection with federal agencies, laws, and permits (Antiquities Act, Reservoir Salvage Act, Section 110 of NHPA, ARPA). It also applies to the collections and the generated data, or associated records and is applicable to both new and preexisting collections

Associated records are defined as "Original records (or copies thereof) that are prepared, assembled and document efforts to locate, evaluate, record, study, preserve or recover a prehistoric or historic resource. Some records such as field notes, artifact inventories, and oral histories may be originals that are prepared as a result of the fieldwork, analysis and report preparation. Other records such as deeds, survey plats, historical maps, and diaries may be copies of original public or archival documents that are assembled and studied as a result of historical research (36 CFR Part 79.4.a.2)."

These guidelines are provided so future materials can be processed and included in the collection in a systematic fashion. Staff may also use this procedure for materials already in their possession in preparation for the materials being accessioned or registered by the archivist under the park museum collection accountability system, the National Park Service Automated National Cataloging System (ANCS+). Accessioning is the preliminary step in identifying collections that will later be cataloged and processed to NPS archival standards. Eventually, finding aids are created to enable staff and researchers to easily access information in the collection archives.

Staff cooperation in carrying out this SOP will greatly accelerate the rate at which materials are processed. Subject matter specialists involved in the creation of these materials carry the greater knowledge about these collections. The quality of the final product will depend upon the quality of staff involvement in the process of identifying the exact nature of archival materials.

Checklist for Preparing Field Documentation

1) Obtain an accession number from the park curator at the commencement of all new field projects.

2) Label ALL materials with the project accession number. Use a soft lead pencil for marking documents or files and a Mylar marking pen for Mylar enclosures such as slide, print or negative sleeves.

3) Materials must be arranged by material type such as field notes, reports, maps, correspondence, photographs, etc. Each group of materials should be stored in individual folders or acceptable archival enclosures.

4) Resource management staff is responsible for turning over all project documentation to the park curator upon completion of a project. In the interest of preserving institutional knowledge, leave collections in their original order. Original order means the organization system created by the originator of a document collection. Resist the urge to take important documents from these collections. If something is needed for future use, copy it or request that the curator make a copy. After copying, replace the document or photo where it was found. Much information about past projects has been lost because collections has been picked apart. Remember these materials will always be available. That is the whole point behind establishing archives.

5) When the archival documentation is transferred to the park museum, the form below should be provided. This form includes the project title, principal investigator, date of project and a history of the project. The name of the individual who obtained the accession number should also be listed. The type and quantity of documentation would be included as well, such as maps (13), field notes (4 notebooks), Correspondence (3 files).

Project Identification Sheet (Use one sheet for each project)

Accession No: _____ (Assigned only by Curator)

Your name, title, office: _____

Project Title _____

Principle Investigator and position during project. Please list staff who might have aided in the project implementation.

_____

Researcher's office location and extension, or current address, occupation, and employer or contact number.

_____

Type and quantity of materials in collection(s) (specimens, papers, files, reports, data, maps, photo prints/negatives/slides, computer media - format/software?) Condition. (i.e. infested, torn, broken, good) Attach additional paper if necessary.

_____

Scope of Project:

Is this collection part of an ongoing project to be updated annually?   Yes ____ No ____
Research goals or project purpose and published or in-house reports to which collection relates

_____

_____

Abstract of collection content. Keywords referring to geographical locations, processes, data types, associated projects. Indicate whether specimens/objects were collected. Attach additional paper if necessary.

_____

_____

Planning for the Curation of Resource Management Records

Records in the Field

Anticipate the kinds of documents that will be needed in the field to record data and use archival materials to produce them (e.g., field excavation forms, field notes, photographic logs, transit data, maps, level records, and videotape). Use archival quality materials in the field. This can reduce the cost of copying information onto archival quality media later. Remember that documentation on electronic media alone is not sufficient because of the lack of long-term stability of these media and their contents.

The records created in the field, as well as in the lab, are vulnerable to insects, vermin, mold, humidity, light, temperature changes, and mishandling. They are also vulnerable to a variety of environmental threats, such as roof leaks, flooding, fire, and asbestos problems, and to theft or other malicious action. The following are a number of general recommendations to follow in the field and lab in order to promote the long-term preservation and viability of the great variety of records created:

- Use appropriate long-lived media for all record types.
- Use permanent and archival stock in paper, ink, lead pencil, folders, and boxes.
- Inspect and redo damaged or inadequate records.
- Label everything, or their containers.
- Use appropriate storage for all media in the field in order to protect them from poor environmental conditions and threat of fire or theft.
- Carefully consider existing guidelines and equipment for digital and audiovisual media, make sure backup copies and hard copy printouts exist, and migrate data to updated software on a regular schedule.
- Ensure that project information and data is captured by appropriately knowledgeable staff.
- Paper records

A number of conservation principles should also be considered for each of the primary types of media used for associated records.

- Use high alpha cellulose, lignin free, acid-free paper, especially for field notebooks, and standardized forms.
- Record information using archival (permanent carbon) inks or #4 (HH) pencils.
- Protect paper from water and humidity, and minimize its exposure to light.
- Try not to fold or roll paper.
- Store papers in archival folders in polyethylene boxes.

Photographs

- Protect all photographic materials (e.g., film, prints, slides, negatives, and transparencies) from heat, rain, and wind. Store them in archival folders in polyethylene boxes.
- Maintain a log of all photographic images.
- Only handle photos along their edges. Do not touch the image with bare fingers.
- Do not use paper or plastic clips, rubber bands, pressure sensitive tape, adhesive or pressure sensitive labels, or Post-it® notes directly on photographs.
- Do not put photographic materials, except unused film, in cold storage without reformatting them for access and duplication.

Magnetic Records

- Protect all magnetic materials (e.g., audio tapes, video tapes) from heat, dust, and dirt.
- Consider the equipment required to play the audiovisual material and the longevity of that equipment.
- Label all records in a permanent, carbon-based ink.
- Store the records in their cases in polyethylene boxes.

Cartographic and Oversized Records

- Oversized records should be stored flat in folders, preferably in map cases. Do not roll or fold.
- Protect paper from water and minimize its exposure to light.

- During storage and use, protect oversized records from tears and rips. Do not use tape to repair tears.
- Label the oversized folders in permanent, carbon-based ink.

Digital Records and Data

- Produce your master records in uncompressed TIF format, if possible. Avoid using proprietary file formats or lossy compression.
- Protect all digital records from heat, dust, dirt, and ultraviolet radiation.
- Choose a storage medium that is considered a standard and research its longevity.
- Keep digital records away from magnetic or electric fields that are created by old telephones, static, and field and lab equipment such as magnetometers and 12-volt transformers. Computer diskettes can be partially or completely erased by such exposure.
- Label the records in permanent, carbon-based ink.

Attachment A: Five Phases of Managing Archival Collections

(From "Museum Archives and Manuscript Collections," *NPS Museum Handbook,* Part II, Appendix D)

Phase 1: Gain Preliminary Control over the Park Records

Survey and describe collections; identify official/non-official records; appraise collections and check them against the Scope of Collection Statement (SOCS); accession collections; order supplies.

Phase 2: Preserve the Park Collections

Conduct the Collection Condition Survey; write treatment or reformatting recommendations; contract to conserve or reformat; re-house; prepare storage, work, and reading room spaces.

Phase 3: Arrange and Describe the Park Collections

Arrange collections; create folder lists; edit and index folder lists; update collection-level survey description; produce finding aids; catalog collections into the Automated National Catalog System (ANCS+).

Phase 4: Refine the Archival Processing

Locate resources; prepare processing plan and documentation strategy; develop a guide to collections; publicize collections.

Phase 5: Provide Access to Park Collections

Review restrictions; write access and usage policies; provide reference service.

Attachment B: Sample Archival and Manuscript Collections Survey Form

(From "Museum Archives and Manuscript Collections," *NPS Museum Handbook*, Part II, Appendix D), US Department of the Interior, National Park Service

COLLECTION TITLE (Creator / Format / Alternate Names/Accession/Catalog #s): Asa Thomas Papers DRTO-00008

DATES (Inclusive & Bulk): 1850-1925; bulk 1860-69

PROVENANCE (Creator / Function / Ownership and Usage History/Related Collections/Language): Asa Thomas (1830-1930) an American engineer, inventor, and explorer specializing in hydraulics created this collection as a record of his life, family, and employment history. Captions on some photos are in Spanish. Note: Must locate a biography of Thomas for the Collection-Level Survey Description. Check the *Who's Who in Science*. This collection was given by Thomas's third wife, Eva Bebernicht Thomas, to their son, Martin Thomas in 1930. Martin Thomas left it to his only daughter Susan Brabb, who gave it to the Park in 1976.

PHYSICAL DESCRIPTION (Linear feet / Item count / Processes / Formats / Genres):45 linear feet of papers including 15 diaries (1850-1925), 63 albums and scrapbooks, 10 lf of correspondence, and 2,000 blueprints.

SUBJECTS (Personal / Group / Taxonomic / Place Names / Eras / Activities / Events / Objects / Structures / Genres): This collection documents the life, family, inventions, instructions, and professional activities of Asa Thomas including engineering projects in the Dry Tortugas, the 1873 world tour, and hydraulic pump inventions.

ARRANGEMENT (Series/Principle of Arrangement / Finding Aid): Into four series by type of document: correspondence, diaries, albums and scrapbooks, and blueprints.

RESTRICTIONS (Check and Describe) Donor _____
Privacy/Publicity _____ Copyright __X__ Libel _____ No Release Forms _____ Archeological, Cave, or Well Site _____ Endangered Species Site _____ Sensitive _____ Classified _____

Fragile _____ Health Hazard _____ Other _____ The donor, A. Thomas's son Marvin, did not donate all copyrights. The papers are unpublished. Some inventions are patented.

LOCATIONS Building(s), Room(s), Walls(s), Shelf Unit(s), Position(s), Box(es): B6 R5 W2 S1-3, B1-40

EVALUATION (Check and Describe Status) Official Records _____ Non-Official Records _____ Fits Park SOCS _____ Outside SOCS _____ (Rate Collection Value: 1=Low; 3=Average; 6=High) Informational __6__ Artifactual __6__ Associational __6__ Evidential __3__ Administrative __3__ Monetary __1__

CONDITION (Check and Describe) Excellent _____ Good __X__ Fair _____ Poor _____ Mold _____ Rodents _____ Insects _____ Nitrate _____ Asbestos _____ Water Damage __X__ Other _____

OTHER (Please Describe)

Appendix H — Suggested Collections Access Policies

National Park Service policy dictates that Park-specific cultural and natural collections be available for educational and scholarly purposes. The NPS is also charged to manage these resources for optimum preservation. To minimize the potential impact on the archives and museum collections and to ensure basic security and preservation conditions, access must be documented, restricted, and monitored. The guidelines in this appendix are followed at [name of Park] in order to provide supervised management of Park-specific resources.

Levels of Access to the Archives and Museum Collections

All serious research—regardless of educational level—is encouraged.

Providing different levels of access to collections is a standard curatorial philosophy underlying the policies of most major museums. Based on the information provided on the research application (included in this appendix), individuals will be provided access to different types of collections information or material depending on their needs and available staff time.

Conditions for Access

- The research application must be completed; it will be used as a basis for determining the level of access necessary, and to maintain a record of use for statistical purposes.

- Level of access will be determined by the chief of natural and cultural resource management and/or the collections manager(s). Prior to allowing direct access to the archives and collections, alternatives such as access to exhibits, publications, photographs, and catalog data will be considered.

- Access will be made with the assistance of the curatorial staff, during regular staff working hours. A fee to cover the cost of staff overtime may be required for access outside of the normal working hours.

- Individuals provided access to archives and collections in nonpublic areas are required to sign in and out using the guest register.

- The "Guidelines for the Use of Archival and Museum Collections" will be followed by all individuals with access to the collections.

- While no user fee will be required for access to the archives or museum collections, the chief of natural and cultural resource management and the curatorial staff will determine what services may be reasonably offered and what charges may be required for services such as staff overtime, photography of specimens, or reproduction of documents.

- All photography of specimens and duplication of documents will take place on-site using the "Guidelines for Photography of Museum Collections and Duplication of Historic Documents."

- A limited amount of space is available for researcher use of archives and museum collections. Researchers are required to check in all collections and remove all personal possessions each evening.

- [Name of Park] reserves the right to request copies of notes made by researchers, and requires copies of research papers or publications resulting in whole or part from use of the collections.

- There may be legal considerations (such as the Native American Graves Protection and Repatriation Act, 1991) which allow or limit access to part of the archives and museum collections.

Access Policy Administration

This statement of policies and procedures is public information, and is available upon request from the following:

Superintendent

[Name of Park]

[Address of Park]

Implementation of these policies and procedures has been delegated to the collections manager(s); however, the superintendent has the final authority to grant access to the archives and museum collections.

The evaluation of requests should consider the motives of the researcher, the projected length of the project, the demands upon the available space, staff, and collections, and the possible benefits of the research project. Access may be denied if thought not to be in the best interests of the resources, the Park, or the National Park Service. Presumably, the chief of natural and cultural resources management will make these decisions in consultation with the collections manager(s).

With increased attention and use, the archives and collections will require increased monitoring to provide security, to detect developing preservation problems, and to facilitate prompt treatment. Regular inventory of the most heavily used portions of the archives and museum collections will be required to ascertain object location and condition.

Research Application for Museum Collections and Historic Documents

[Name of Park]

Name _____ Telephone Number (____)_____

Institution/Organization _____

Address _____

Date you wish to visit _____

(An alternate date might be necessary due to staffing limitations.)

Have you previously conducted research in the Park's museum collection?   Yes___ No_____

Research topic and materials you wish to see

_____

Indicate which activities you wish to do

☐ Consult catalog cards   ☐ Consult archeological records

☐ View objects in storage   ☐ Study objects in storage

☐ Draw objects   ☐ Consult historic documents

☐ Other _____

Purpose of your research

☐ Book   ☐ Article

☐ Lecture/conference paper   ☐ Term paper

☐ Thesis   ☐ Dissertation

☐ Exhibit   ☐ Project

☐ Identify/compare with other material

☐ Other commercial use or distribution _____

☐ Other _____

I have read the Museum Collection Access and Use/Research Policies and Procedures and agree to abide by it and all rules and regulations of [name of Park]. I agree to exercise all due care in handling any object in the museum collection and assume full responsibility for any damage, accidental or otherwise, which I might inflict upon any museum property. Violation of National Park Service rules and regulations may forfeit research privileges.

Signature _____

Date _____

Please return to: Curator, [Name of Park], National Park Service, [Address of Park]

(reverse side: Research Application)

National Park Service Use Only

Identification (provide at least one)
Institutional ID _____
Driver's License Number _____

Research Topic
_____
_____

Location of Research (check one)
☐ Curatorial Office

☐ Storage

☐ Exhibit Area

☐ Others _____

Museum Objects Reviewed by the Researcher

[Name of Park]

Park	Catalog	Object Name	Location	Accession	Acronym	Number

Approved by:

Name _____

Title _____

Date _____

Guidelines for the Use of Archival and Museum Collections

[Name of Park]

The guidelines provided here are followed at [name of Park] regarding use of the Park's museum collections and archives. It should be noted that these resources are separate from the Park's library, which is managed by [insert name].

It is the policy of the National Park Service that its museum collections and archival resources be available for educational and scholarly purposes. The NPS is also charged with managing these resources for optimum preservation. To minimize impact on these collections, it is necessary to regulate access to the materials.

Copies of the research application and the full text of the "Guidelines for the Use of Archival and Museum Collections" are available to the public, upon request from:

Superintendent,

[Name of Park]

[Address of Park]

Availability

The museum collections and archives are open Monday through Friday, from 8:00 A.M. to 4:30 P.M. Park staff should contact the Park collections manager(s) for assistance with access. The museum collections and archives are "non-lending," and the materials will remain in the building.

Non-staff users must complete a research application (included in this appendix) prior to accessing information or materials to ensure that assistance is available upon arrival. Access will not normally be granted on weekends. All materials must stay within the study areas provided within the collection management facility. The size and location of these areas may vary according to the time of year, requests from other researchers, and staff available. The researcher may bring only those materials needed for research into the assigned study area.

Registration

The Guest Register, used to record access to museum and archival collections, must be signed when the collections are used by staff or non-staff members. Non-staff researchers are required to complete a Research Application (included with this policy). These forms will be retained indefinitely for statistical analysis and as a permanent record of collections use. A new application is required for each research project, and must be renewed each calendar year.

As part of the registration process, the researcher will be given a copy of these procedures to review and sign, thereby indicating his/her agreement to abide by them.

Use of Archival Records and Manuscripts

Many of the Park administrative records, archeological records, and other historic reference material have been copied onto microfiche, and a reader/printer is available for limited research use by the public. Where microfiche is available, it will be used for research requests. Only in the most extraordinary circumstances will original documents be used when microfiche is available.

When microfiche is *not* available, the archives user should follow these procedures to ensure careful handling of all materials:

- Remove only one folder from a box at a time. Do not remove or alter the arrangement of materials in the folders.

- Maintain the exact order of materials in a folder, as well as folders within a box. If a mistake in arrangement is discovered, please bring it to the attention of museum staff. Do not rearrange material yourself.

- Do not erase existing marks on documents and do not add any additional marks.

- Do not lean on, write on, trace, fold, or handle materials in any way that may damage them.

- Use only pencils for note-taking. The use of pens of any kind is prohibited. Typewriters and computers may be used for note-taking if provided by the researcher.

Duplication

The Park will consider requests for limited reproduction of materials when it can be done without injury to the records and when it does not violate donor agreements or copyright restrictions. Depending on the number of copies requested, there may be a charge for photocopying. Fragile documents and bound volumes will not be photocopied. All photocopying of archival material is to be done by the museum staff.

Copyrights and Citations

The revised copyright law, which took effect in 1978, provides protection for unpublished material for the life of the author, plus 70 years. In addition, all unpublished material created prior to 1978, except that in the public domain, is protected at least through the year 2002. Permission to duplicate does not constitute permission to publish. The researcher accepts full legal responsibility for observing the copyright law, as well as the laws of defamation, privacy, and publicity rights.

Information obtained from the Park museum collections and archives must be properly cited, in both publications and unpublished papers. The citation should read:

"(Object name and catalog #) in the collection of [name of Park]. Photograph courtesy of the National Park Service."

Restrictions on Use

The use of certain materials may be restricted by statute, by the creator, or by the donor. For the protection of its collections, the Park also reserves the right to restrict access to material that is not fully processed, or is exceptionally valuable or fragile, and to information that may be restricted or confidential in nature.

Responding to Off-Site Reference Inquiries

It is the responsibility of the Park curatorial staff to attempt to answer inquiries received by letter or telephone within at least 20 days from the date of receipt. Clearly, the extent to which this reference service is undertaken will depend upon availability of staff time and the nature of the question. The receipt of written inquiries will be acknowledged by telephone if a full response cannot be provided promptly. The staff must set time limits for answering research questions, so researchers are encouraged to use the collections in person.

A record of all research inquiries will be maintained. Such a record is useful for security and for compiling statistics on research use of the collection. Use of the collections by Park staff will be included in these statistics.

Guidelines for Handling Museum Collections

Handling museum collections may be hazardous. Follow the guidelines provided here to ensure safe handling.

Archeological collections can contain broken glass and rusty metal objects with sharp edges. Historic material may retain chemical or biological contamination. Natural history collections contain chemical preservatives and possible biological contamination. Archival collections may be contaminated with mold, insects, and vermin droppings, or may contain asbestos or cellulose nitrate film.

- Use caution in handling collections, and wear gloves when requested to do so.

- Curatorial personnel will retrieve and replace material for anyone using the collections. Direct access to material may be restricted if the object is very fragile.

- Do not remove materials from storage packaging without the permission and assistance of the curatorial staff. The packaging is necessary to prevent damage and deterioration of the specimen, and to protect the researcher from potential injury.

- Always handle objects with clean hands. Use white cotton gloves when handling metal, photographs, paper, and leather objects; washed white duck gardener's gloves may be required for heavy objects.

- Do **not** use white cotton gloves when handling glass or other objects with slippery surfaces, very heavy objects, or items with friable or brittle surfaces.

- Do not pick up anything before you have a place to put it down and your path to this place is clear.

- Look over an artifact before lifting it to see how it is stored and to observe any peculiarities of its construction, fragility, etc. If an object is made in separable sections, take it apart before moving it. Do not attempt to carry heavy or awkward objects alone. Never carry more than one object at a time, and be particularly careful with long objects.

- Except for small items, always grasp an object with two hands, and grasp the largest part or body of the object. Slide one hand under fragile items as you lift them.

- If an artifact has a weak or damaged area, place or store it with that area visible.

Special Objects

- Mounted herbarium specimens should be laid on a flat surface and the folder cover and specimens handled gently, taking care not to bend the sheets or touch the actual specimen.
- Pinned insect specimens should be handled as little as possible, and then handled by the pin. Avoid bumping and strong drafts when handling these specimens.
- Skulls and skeletons should be kept in their jars or containers while examining.
- Ceramics and baskets should be supported from the bottom, never lifted by the rim or handles.
- Photographs, transparencies and negatives should be handled by the edges, and should remain in protective Mylar sleeves whenever possible. White gloves should always be used when handling photographs.
- Unrolled textiles should be broadly supported from underneath rather than by holding from the edge.

Reporting Damage

Please report any damage you observe or cause to specimens.

Behavior

- Food, beverages, smoking, and pets are not allowed in the storage or study areas.
- Staff members are responsible for the behavior of any person accompanying them into the collections.
- Children under six years of age must be accompanied by an adult and physically controlled at all times. Other minors must be under the direct supervision of an accompanying adult at all times.

I have read and understand the above policy.

Name _____ Date _____

Guidelines for Photography of Collections and Duplication of Historic Documents

[NAME OF PARK]

This policy documents appropriate procedures for providing photographs of [name of Park] National Park museum collections, and for duplicating original historic photographs and documents. The policy is intended to prevent damage or loss through mishandling or exposure to detrimental environmental conditions.

Duplicate Photographs of Museum Collections

There are many possible uses for photographs of the items in museum collections, the most common being exhibits, publication, and research. It is the policy of the National Park Service to encourage the use of NPS collections in these legitimate ventures and to make photographs of museum collections available within reasonable limitations.

Photography involves exposing often fragile museum objects to potential damage or loss from handling and exposure to heat and light. The NPS minimizes this potential damage by photographing items as few times as possible. To accomplish this, the Park will develop a reference collection of object photographs that will be available for public use. A minimal fee may be required for copies of the photographs.

In order to provide this service, and to build the necessary reference collection, the following procedures will be followed:

- Requests for photographs of items in the museum collections will be submitted to the Park curator, who will establish any necessary priority for the work. Requests should be made on copies of the attached form.

- Requested items that do not have copy negatives will be photographed based on these priorities. A cost recovery charge for photography and processing may be required.

- Photography will be done at the Park, under Park control, to preclude the possibility of artifact damage or loss. The resulting photographic negatives and their copyrights belong to the National Park Service.

- Once an object has been photographed, the negative will be maintained at the Park to fill future requests for photographs of that object. A minimal cost recovery charge through the Park Association maybe required for prints.

Duplication of Historic Photographs and Documents

All historic photographic processes and document types are subject to rapid deterioration from exposure to visible light and are very susceptible to damage from handling. Handling is often disastrous to these materials and causes damage such as tears, cracks, abrasions, fingerprints and stains. Handling also subjects historic photographs and documents to frequent fluctuations in temperature and humidity.

To prevent further deterioration, copies will be made of all historic photographs and documents, with the copy replacing the originals as the primary item for research and use. The original material will remain in storage, for the most part, as primary source material.

Increased requests for access to and copies of historic photographs and documents will require the following procedures to establish priorities for the duplication work:

- Requests for duplicate historic photographs and documents are submitted to the Park collections manager who will establish any necessary priority for copy work.

- Requested items that do not presently have copy negatives will be duplicated based on these priorities. The originals must be accessioned and cataloged into the Park collection. A cost recovery charge for duplication may be requested.

- Duplication will be done at the Park, or under Park control, to preclude possibilities of loss or damage of the originals.

- Once the photographs have been duplicated, copy prints and modern negatives of the originals will be maintained and used for intellectual access and for further duplication. Microfiche copies of historic documents will also be maintained and will be available for use. A cost recovery charge may be required for copy prints.

The Park will provide the sufficient quality duplication necessary to fulfill all the normal requirements for suitable reproduction. Outside individuals or organizations that request use of the images will be required to use only those copies provided by the Park; and they will be obligated to acknowledge NPS credit if the photographs are published or exhibited to the public. By law, users must also credit the photographer, if known.

Request for Photographs of Items from the Museum Collections

[Name of Park]

Catalog #	Object Name	B&W/Color	Size	Finish

The undersigned agrees to provide the following credit statement for all publication use:

"(object name and catalog #) in the collection of [name of Park]. Photograph courtesy of the National Park Service."

Signature _____

Date _____

John Day Fossil Beds National Monument

Bibliography

Beckham, Stephen Dow, with Florence K. Lentz. *Rocks and Hard Places: Historic Resources Study, John Day Fossil Beds National Monument.* Seattle, WA: U.S. Department of the Interior, National Park Service, Pacific Northwest Regional Library, 2000.

Cogswell, Marilee, Cathleen Frank, and Linda Rhines, comp. *Legislative History for John Day Fossil Beds National Monument.* Seattle, WA: National Park Service, Pacific Northwest Regional Library, 1985.

Mark, Stephen R. *Floating in the Stream of Time: An Administrative History of John Day Fossil Beds National Monument.* Seattle: U.S. Department of the Interior, National Park Service, Pacific West Field Area, Columbia Cascades Cluster, 1995.

National Park Service. *Integrated Pest Management Plan, John Day Fossil Beds National Monument.* Kimberly, OR: U.S. Department of the Interior, National Park Service, 2006.

National Park Service. *Integrated Pest Management Plan, John Day Fossil Beds National Monument.* Kimberly, OR: U.S. Department of the Interior, National Park Service, 2002.

National Park Service. *Resource Management Plan, John Day Fossil Beds National Monument.* Kimberly, OR: U.S. Department of the Interior, National Park Service, 1993.

National Park Service. *Resources Management Plan and Environmental Assessment, Statement for Management, John Day Fossil Beds National Monument.* Kimberly, OR: U.S. Department of the Interior, National Park Service, Pacific Northwest Region, 1992.

National Park Service. *Resources Management Plan and Environmental Assessment, John Day Fossil Beds National Monument.* Kimberly,

OR: U.S. Department of the Interior, National Park Service, Pacific Northwest Region, 1992.

National Park Service. *Statement for Management, John Day Fossil Beds National Monument.* Kimberly, OR: U.S. Department of the Interior, National Park Service, Pacific Northwest Region, 1992.

National Park Service. *Draft General Management Plan/Environmental Impact Statement, John Day Fossil Beds National Monument [Park Review].* Denver, CO: U.S. Department of the Interior, National Park Service, 2007.

National Park Service. *Paleontological Research Plan, John Day Fossil Beds National Monument.* Kimberly, OR: U.S. Department of the Interior, National Park Service, 1989.

National Park Service. *General Management Plan, John Day Fossil Beds National Monument.* Denver, CO: U.S. Department of the Interior, National Park Service, 1979.

National Park Service. *John Day Fossil Beds National Monument Business Plan.* Kimberly, OR: U.S. Department of the Interior, National Park Service, 2006.

PPI Exhibit Design and Fabrication. *Historic Cant Ranch House Exhibits: General Maintenance Guidebook.* Portland, OR: PPI Exhibit Design and Fabrication, ca 2004.

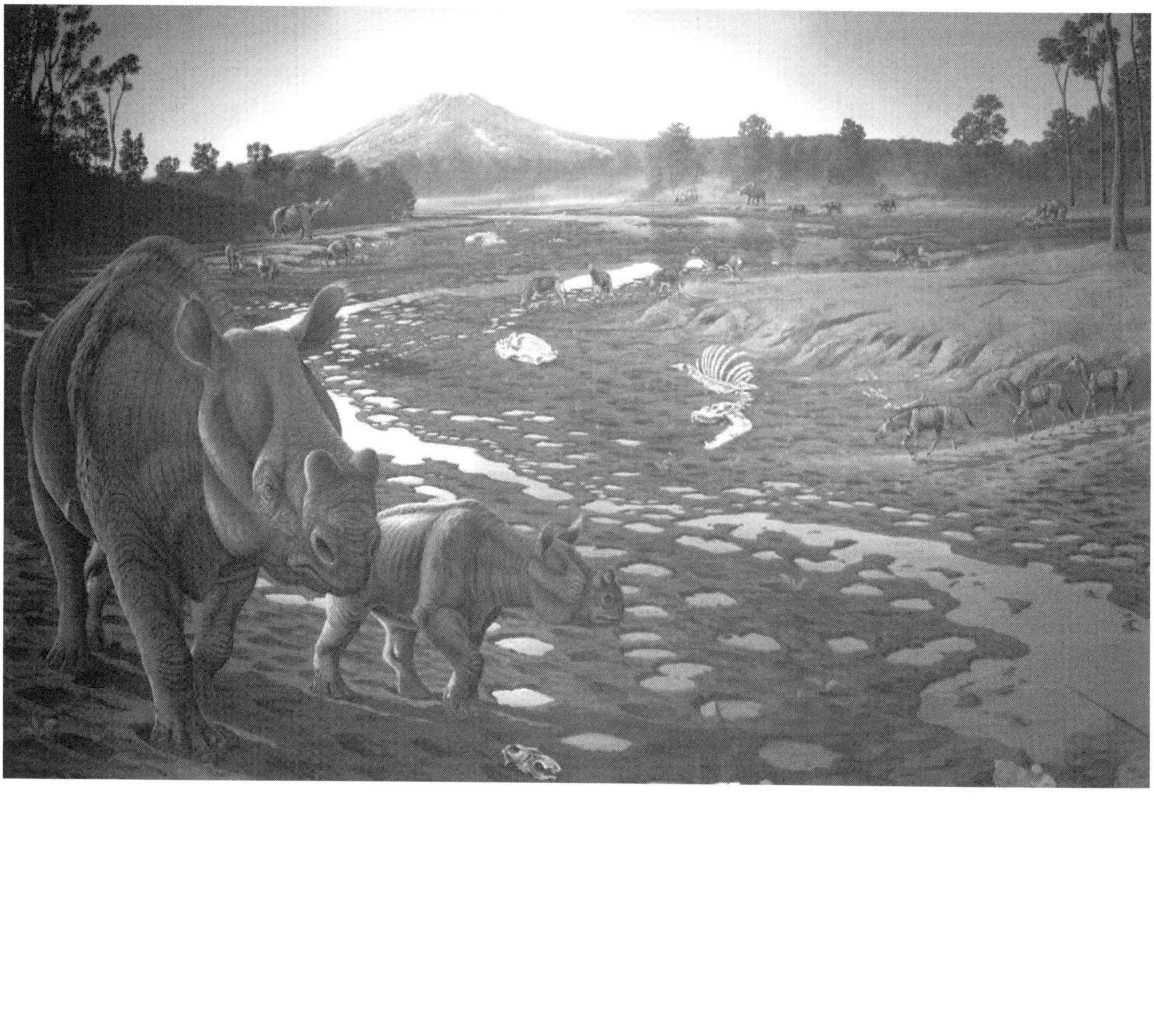

Made in the USA
San Bernardino, CA
25 January 2014